LANDLORD AND TENANT SERIES

The Tenants' Right of Pre-emption

LANDLORD AND TENANT SERIES

The Tenants' Right of Pre-emption

The Right of First Refusal under the Landlord and Tenant Act 1987, Part I

by

Professor Phillip Kenny, LLM, Solicitor

Head of School of Law, University of Northumbria
at Newcastle

With Forms Contributed by Nigel Emmerson Esq
Solicitor of Messrs Dickinson Dees, Newcastle upon Tyne

BLACKSTONE PRESS LIMITED

*This book has been printed digitally and produced in a standard specification
in order to ensure its continuing availability*

OXFORD
UNIVERSITY PRESS

Great Clarendon Street, Oxford OX2 6DP

Oxford University Press is a department of the University of Oxford.
It furthers the University's objective of excellence in research, scholarship,
and education by publishing worldwide in

Oxford New York

Auckland   Cape Town Dar es Salaam   Hong Kong   Karachi
Kuala Lumpur Madrid Melbourne Mexico City   Nairobi
New Delhi Shanghai Taipei Toronto
With offices in
Argentina Austria Brazil Chile Czech Republic France Greece
Guatemala Hungary Italy Japan South Korea Poland Portugal
Singapore Switzerland Thailand Turkey Ukraine Vietnam

Oxford is a registered trade mark of Oxford University Press
in the UK and in certain other countries

Published in the United States
by Oxford University Press Inc., New York

A Blackstone Press book
© Professor Phillip Kenny, 1999

ISBN 1-85431-980-9

Antony Rowe Ltd., Eastbourne

Contents

Preface ix

Abbreviations x

Table of Cases xi

Table of Statutes xiii

Table of Secondary Legislation xix

1 Application of the Act 1

1.1 Introduction   1.2 Identifying how the Act applies   1.3 Premises to which the Act applies   1.4 Land and other rights associated with building   1.5 Buildings with a mixed use   1.6 Land held under different titles   1.7 Application to estates including more than one building   1.8 Landlord   1.9 Sub-tenancy situations   1.10 Application to sub-sales   1.10 Application to sub-sales   1.11 Qualifying tenant   1.12 Multiple flat holders   1.13 Relevant disposals   1.14 Excepted disposals   1.15 Application to contracts and options

2 The Offer Notices 20

2.1 The offer notice   2.2 Disposal of several buildings   2.3 Service of the offer notice   2.4 Method of service of notices   2.5 Section 5A offer notice:

where disposal is a contract to create or transfer an estate or interest in land 2.6 Section 5B offer notice in cases of sale by auction 2.7 Section 5C offer notice: grant of an option or right of pre-emption 2.8 Section 5D offer notice: cases where conveyance not preceded by contract 2.9 Section 5E offer notice: where there is a disposal for non-monetary consideration

3 Further Procedures 29

3.1 Acceptance of landlord's offer 3.2 Requisite majority of qualifying tenants 3.3 The nominated person 3.4 Failure by tenants to accept offer or make nomination 3.5 What can be disposed of? 3.6 Procedure after a tenants' purchaser is nominated 3.7 Assignment covenants 3.8 Once there is a binding contract 3.9 Lapse of landlord's offer

4 Enforcement Against Purchasers 38

4.1 Introduction 4.2 Right to information 4.3 Compliance by purchaser 4.4 Right to take benefit of certain transactions 4.5 Time for exercise of right 4.6 Section 12A notices: taking the benefit of a contract 4.7 Section 12B notices: right to compel sale etc. by purchaser 4.8 Section 12C notices: surrender by landlord 4.9 Disputes before leasehold valuation tribunals 4.10 Rights of qualifying tenants against subsequent purchaser 4.11 Termination of rights against purchaser 4.12 Prospective purchaser notice 4.13 Enforement of the Act 4.14 Tenants' rights as property rights

5 Avoidance and Criminal Offences 54

5.1 Criminal offences 5.2 Methods of avoiding the Act

6 Litigation 59

6.1 Introduction 6.2 Leasehold valuation tribunal 6.3 Applications to the court

Appendix A: Landlord and Tenant Act 1987 63

Appendix B: Forms for use under the Landlord and Tenant Act 1987, Part I 103

Form 1 — Section 5A notice by the landlord to the tenants in case of sale by contract to be completed by conveyance

Form 2 — Section 5A notice by the landlord to the tenants in case of sale by contract to be completed by conveyance

Form 3 — Section 5B notice by the landlord to the tenants in case of sale by auction

Form 4 — Section 5C notice by the landlord to the tenants in case of grant of option or right of pre-emption

Form 5 — Section 5D notice by the landlord to the tenants in case of a conveyance not preceded by contract, option or right of pre-emption binding on the landlord

Form 6 — Section 5E notice by the landlord to the tenants in case of disposal for non-monetary consideration

Form 7 — Section 6(3) notice by the requisite majority of qualifying tenants of acceptance

Form 8 — Section 6(5) notice by the qualifying tenants to the landlord informing the landlord of the nominated person

Form 9 — Section 8(3)(a) notice by the landlord to the nominated person of withdrawal by the landlord from the transaction

Form 10 — Section 8A(4)(a) notice by the nominated person to the landlord of withdrawal by the nominated person from the transaction

Form 11 — Section 8B(2) notice by the nominated person to the landlord of acceptance of the provisions of section 8B

Form 12 — Section 8B(4)(a) notice by the nominated person to the landlord of acceptance of the terms of the auction contract

Form 13 — Section 8C(2) notice by the requisite majority of qualifying tenants of acceptance of an offer of disposal for non-monetary consideration

Form 14 — Section 8E(3) notice by the landlord to the nominated person stating that the landlord has discharged its duty under section 8E of the Act

Form 15 — Section [9A(1) and 14(1)] notice by the nominated person to the landlord of withdrawal by the nominated person from the transaction

Form 16 — Section 9B(1) notice by the landlord to the nominated person of withdrawal

Form 17 — Section 10(1) notice by the landlord to the qualifying tenants stating that the property has ceased to be within the Act

Form 18 — Section 11A(1) notice by the requisite majority of qualifying tenants to a purchaser

Form 19 — Section 12A notice by the requisite majority of qualifying tenants to the landlord

Form 20 — Section 12B(2) purchase notice

Form 21 — Section 12C(2) notice by the requisite majority of qualifying tenants to a purchaser requiring new tenancy

Form 22 — Section 16(3)(a) notice by the purchaser to the subsequent purchaser

Form 23 — Section 16(3)(b) notice by the purchaser to the nominated person

Form 24 — Section 16(2)(a) notice by the purchaser to the tenants

Form 25 — Section 17 notice by the purchaser to the tenants that Act has ceased to apply

Form 26 — Section 5B(8) notice by the landlord informing the tenants of the particulars of the auction

Form 27 — Section 18(1) notice by the prospective purchaser to the qualifying tenants

Appendix C: The Corresponding Date Rule   152

Appendix D: Landlord and Tenant Act 1985, s. 3A   154

Index   156

Preface

This book is concerned with a small piece of legislation – the Landlord and Tenant Act 1987, Part I, as amended by the Housing Act 1996. It was in 1987 a shockingly badly drafted piece of legislation, and as amended remains a front-runner in any possible competition for ill-conceived legislation. The Act has caused me more difficulty in its application than any other I have considered, including the astonishingly opaque attempts of the gifted illusionists who draft VAT legislation – if indeed these strange pieces of prose have human progenitors.

Part I of the 1987 Act affects two characters – the landlord which owns blocks of flats and the tenants who dwell in them. The purpose of the legislation is to allow tenants the chance to take over the management should the landlord dispose of its interest. In general the landlord in question is a property company with access to specialist legal advice. It is supposed by some that the tenant is a babe lost in the dense woods of property law. Consequently, the cost order-free forum of the leasehold valuation tribunal is available at times to the tenant, though curiously most disputes require resolution in the more rarefied atmosphere of the civil courts where legal refinement exacts its due price from those who importune its favours. From time to time those such as myself, ekeing out a living as scavengers in the dust-heaps of our law, mutter a silent prayer to the kindly legislature which creates another mound of legislation. For the lawyer asked to sieve through the spoil-heap of this Act it is indeed a Golden Mound.

Phillip Kenny
Newcastle upon Tyne
Spring 1999

Abbreviations

CCR	County Court Rules
LTA 1987	Landlord and Tenant Act 1987
Ord.	Order
para.	paragraph
r.	rule
RSC	Rules of the Supreme Court
s.	section
Sch.	Schedule

Table of Cases

Adams v Lindsell (1881) 1 B and Ald 681   35

Belvedere Court Management Ltd v Frogmore Developments Ltd [1996]
1 All ER 312   12, 44, 46
Box Parish Council v Lacey [1979] 1 All ER 113   26
Brown & Root Technology Ltd v Sun Alliance and London Assurance Co. Ltd [1997]
18 EG 123   39

Chiswell v Griffon Land and Estates [1975] 2 All ER 665   23
Crumpton et al v Unifox Properties Ltd et al (1992) 25 HLR 121   53
Curl v Angelo [1948] 2 All ER 189   6

Denetower Ltd v Toop [1991] 3 All ER 666   3, 42, 43, 44

Fitzpatrick v Sterling Housing Associations Ltd [1997] 4 All ER 991   16

Ground Premium Property Management Ltd v Longmint Ltd [1998] 11 EG 183   43

Harrogate BC v Simpson (1984) 17 HLR 205   16

Kay Green v Twinsectra Ltd [1997] 23 EG 146   43, 44
Kay Green v Twinsectra Ltd [1996] 4 All ER 546   9, 43, 44

Land Securities plc v Receiver for the Metropolitan Police District [1983] 2 All ER 254   26
Leicester PBS v Shearley [1951] Ch 90   57

Mainwaring v Trustees of Henry Smith's Charity [1996] 2 All ER 220   57
Mainwaring v Trustees of Henry Smith's Charity (1996) 28 HLR 584   14, 17
Malpas v St. Ermin's Property Co. Ltd (1992) 24 HLR 537   10
Metropolitan Properties v Barder [1968] 1 All ER 536   6

Michaels v Harley House (Marylebone) Ltd, The Times, 16 March 1997   56

National Provincial Bank v Ainsworth [1965] AC 1125   53

Parkins v Westminster City Council [1998] 13 EG 145   6
Parsons v Trustees of Henry Smith's Charity (1974) 230 EG 1887   6
Polychronakis v Richards, The Independent, 22 October 1997; The Times,
     19 November 1997   55
Pritchard v Briggs [1980] 1 All ER 294   26

R v Hunt [1987] AC 352   55
R v Lincoln (Kesteven) Justices, ex parte O'Connor [1983] Crim LR 621   26

Smith v Seghill Overseers (1875) LR 10 QB 422   13
St Thomas's Hospital (Governors) v Charing Cross Rly Co. (1861) I John & H 400,
     70 ER 802   3
Staszewki v Maribella Ltd [1998] 04 EG 149   39, 40
Street v Mountford [1988] AC 809   13
Stevens v Chown [1901] 1 Ch 894   29

Tandon v Trustees of Spurgeon's Homes [1992] 1 All ER 1086   5
30 Upperton Gardens Management v Akano [1990] 2 EGLR 232   10
Twinsectra Ltd v Jones [1998] 23 EG 134   43, 44, 47

Table of Statutes

Charities Act 1993   95
Children Act 1989
  Sch. 1
    para. 1   66
Companies Act 1985
  s. 736   14, 93

Environmental Protection Act 1990
  s. 80(4)   55
  s. 80(6)   55

Housing Act 1980
  s. 52   12, 64
  Sch. 2
    para. 2   61
Housing Act 1985
  Part V   95
  s. 1   55, 81
  s. 6   94
  s. 79   6
Housing Act 1988   1, 12, 13, 14
  Part I   65
  Part III   94
  s. 1   6
  s. 34   13
  s. 34(1)(c)   14
  Sch. 13   15
Housing Act 1996   ix, 1, 10, 14, 22, 39, 44, 47,
    48, 103, 105, 117, 119, 121, 123, 125, 127,
    128, 129, 130, 131, 132, 134, 135, 136, 137,
    138, 140, 142, 144, 145, 146, 147, 148, 149,
    150
  s. 89   14, 17

Housing Act 1996 — *continued*
  s. 90   56
  s. 91   38
  Sch. 6   9
Housing Associations Act 1958   95

Inheritance (Provision for Family and
    Dependants) Act 1975
  s. 2   15, 66
Interpretation Act 1978
  s. 7   22
  Sch. 5   33

Land Clauses Consolidation Act 1845
  s. 92   3
Land Registration Act 1925
  s. 70   53, 112
  s. 70(1)(g)   53
Landlord and Tenant Act 1954   13
  Part II   13, 64
Landlord and Tenant Act 1985   95
  s. 3   38
  s. 3A   18, 38, 39, 41, 77, 82
  s. 3A(1)–(2)   154
  s. 3A(3)   155
Landlord and Tenant Act 1987   ix, 1, 2, 3, 4,
    5, 7, 8, 9, 10, 11, 12, 13, 14, 17, 18, 21, 22,
    23, 25, 26, 27, 29, 30, 31, 36, 37, 38, 40, 41,
    42, 43, 44, 45, 47, 49, 50, 55, 56, 57, 58,
    63–102, 103, 105, 117, 119, 121, 123, 125,
    127, 128, 129, 130, 131, 132, 134, 135, 136,
    137, 138, 140, 142, 144, 145, 146, 147, 148,
    149, 150, 151

Landlord and Tenant Act 1987 — *continued*
Part I   ix, 1, 3, 4, 11, 16, 23, 38, 44, 45, 48,
    49, 50, 51, 53, 54, 58, 59, 62, 103, 128,
    137, 140, 142, 148, 151, 154
Part III   3, 4, 44
s. 1   43
s. 1(1)   32, 63
s. 1(2)   2, 3, 63
s. 1(2)(a)   2, 7, 12
s. 1(2)(b)–(c)   2
s. 1(3)   2, 7, 8, 63–4
s. 1(4)–(5)   64
s. 2   2, 104, 106, 118, 120, 122, 124, 126,
    127, 128, 129, 130, 131, 133, 134, 135,
    136, 137, 138, 141, 143, 147, 148
s. 2(1)   58, 64
s. 2(1)(a)–(b)   11
s. 2(2)   64
s. 3   12, 104, 106, 118, 120, 121, 122,
    124, 126, 128, 133, 137, 138, 141, 143,
    144
s. 3(1)   2, 64–5
s. 3(2)   2, 14, 58, 65
s. 3(3)   2, 14, 65
s. 3(4)   2, 11, 13, 65
s. 4   2, 32
s. 4(1)   14, 18, 26, 65
s. 4(1)(a)   15
s. 4(1A)   15, 56, 65
s. 4(1)(a)   15
s. 4(1A)   15, 56, 65
s. 4(2)   26, 56, 65–7
s. 4(2)(a)(iii)   15
s. 4(2)(aa)   15
s. 4(2)(b)–(da)   16
s. 4(2)(e)–(h)   16
s. 4(2)(i)   12, 17, 18
s. 4(2)(i)(i)   16
s. 4(2)(i)(ii)   17
s. 4(2)(j)–(k)   16
s. 4(2)(l)   17, 56
s. 4(3)   67
s. 4(3)(b)   16
s. 4(4)   67
s. 4(5)   16, 67
s. 4(5)(b)   16
s. 4(6)   16, 67
s. 4A   14, 17, 26
s. 4A(1)   17, 67–8
s. 4A(1)(a)   55
s. 4A(2)   18, 68
s. 4A(2)(a)–(b)   12
s. 4A(3)–(4)   68
s. 5   1, 3, 9, 17, 18, 20, 21, 22, 25, 27, 30, 52,
    56, 57, 150, 151, 154

Landlord and Tenant Act 1987 — *continued*
s. 5(1)   25, 31, 68, 104, 106, 118, 120, 122,
    124, 126, 133, 137, 139, 141, 143, 144
s. 5(2)   20, 68–9
s. 5(3)   9, 10, 20, 21, 22, 69, 104, 106, 118,
    120, 122, 124, 126, 133, 137, 139, 141,
    143, 144
s. 5(4)   23, 69
s. 5(5)   22, 69
s. 5A   7, 24, 25, 27, 28, 103, 105
s. 5A(1)   69
s. 5A(2)–(3)   24, 69
s. 5A(4)–(6)   24, 70
s. 5B   7, 24, 25, 28, 32, 35, 36, 117
s. 5B(1)   70
s. 5B(2)–(6)   25, 70
s. 5B(7)   70
s. 5B(8)   25, 70, 118, 149
s. 5C   7, 24, 25, 26, 27, 28, 119
s. 5C(1)   71
s. 5C(2)–(5)   27, 71
s. 5D   7, 25, 28, 121
s. 5D(1)–(4)   71
s. 5D(5)   72
s. 5E   7, 20, 25, 28, 123
s. 5E(1)–(3)   72
s. 6   25, 30, 54, 104, 105, 118, 119, 121
s. 6(1)   29, 30, 72
s. 6(1)(b)   30
s. 6(2)   30, 72
s. 6(3)   30, 72, 125
s. 6(3)(b)   30
s. 6(4)   24, 30, 72–3
s. 6(4)(b)   30
s. 6(5)   31, 73, 127
s. 6(6)–(7)   73
s. 7   32, 54
s. 7(1)   73
s. 7(2)–(3)   32, 73
s. 7(4)   32, 73–4
s. 8   18, 54
s. 8(1)–(2)   74
s. 8(3)   33, 74
s. 8(3)(a)   128
s. 8(4)–(5)   74
s. 8A   33
s. 8A(1)   74
s. 8A(2)–(3)   33, 74
s. 8A(4)   34, 74–5
s. 8A(4)(a)   129
s. 8A(4)(b)   34
s. 8A(5)   33, 34, 75
s. 8A(6)   35, 75
s. 8B   130
s. 8B(1)   75

Landlord and Tenant Act 1987 — *continued*
  s. 8B(2)   75, 130
  s. 8B(3)   75
  s. 8B(4)   75
  s. 8B(4)(a)   131
  s. 8B(5)   75
  s. 8B(6)   76
  s. 8C   28, 123, 132
  s. 8C(1)   76
  s. 8C(2)   76, 132
  s. 8C(3)   28, 76
  s. 8C(4)   28, 48, 59, 60, 76
  s. 8D   18, 19
  s. 8D(1)   76–7
  s. 8D(2)   18, 77
  s. 8E   22, 134
  s. 8E(1)–(2)   36, 77
  s. 8E(3)   36, 77, 134
  s. 8E(4)   36, 77–8
  s. 8E(5)   36, 78
  s. 8E(6)   78
  s. 9   54
  s. 9A   33, 36, 135
  s. 9A(1)   34, 78, 135
  s. 9A(2)   37, 78
  s. 9A(3)   78
  s. 9A(4)   34, 35, 78
  s. 9A(5)   34, 78
  s. 9A(5)(a)   35
  s. 9A(6)–(7)   35, 79
  s. 9A(8)   36, 79
  s. 9B   32, 33, 36
  s. 9B(1)   79, 136
  s. 9B(2)   79
  s. 9B(3)   34, 79
  s. 9B(4)   33, 79
  s. 9B(5)   79
  s. 10   36, 37, 54
  s. 10(1)   37, 80, 137
  s. 10(2)   80
  s. 10(3)   37, 80
  s. 10(4)–(5)   80
  s. 10A   22, 29, 32, 38, 54, 55, 56
  s. 10A(1)   80
  s. 10A(2)   81
  s. 10A(3)   55, 81
  s. 10A(3)(a)–(b)   55
  s. 10A(4)   55, 81
  s. 10A(5)   29, 38, 55, 81
  s. 11   18, 28, 39, 40, 123
  s. 11(1)   81
  s. 11(2)   31, 81
  s. 11(3)   81–2, 124, 144, 147, 148
  s. 11A   18, 31, 38, 39, 41, 48, 49, 50, 147,
    148

Landlord and Tenant Act 1987 — *continued*
  s. 11A(1)   82, 138
  s. 11A(1)(a)–(b)   39
  s. 11A(2)   39, 82
  s. 11A(3)   28, 39, 82
  s. 11A(3)(b)   39
  s. 11A(4)   39, 82
  s. 12   3, 4, 18, 28, 43, 44, 97, 123
  s. 12(6)   47
  s. 12A   31, 40, 41, 42–5, 48, 49, 50, 51, 59,
    140, 145
  s. 12A(1)   82
  s. 12A(2)   28, 41, 82–3
  s. 12A(3)   83
  s. 12A(3)(a)   42
  s. 12A(3)(b)   42
  s. 12A(4)   42, 83
  s. 12A(5)   42, 48, 49, 59, 60, 83
  s. 12B   31, 40, 41, 44, 45–7, 48, 49, 50, 51,
    59, 60, 145
  s. 12B(1)   83
  s. 12B(2)   45, 83–4, 142
  s. 12B(3)   28, 41, 84
  s. 12B(4)   45, 48, 49, 59, 60, 84, 141, 143
  s. 12B(5)   46, 84–5
  s. 12B(5)(a)–(b)   46
  s. 12B(6)   46, 85
  s. 12B(7)   47, 85
  s. 12C   31, 40, 41, 44, 47–8, 49, 50, 51, 59,
    60, 145
  s. 12C(1)   85
  s. 12C(2)   85, 144
  s. 12C(3)   41, 85
  s. 12C(4)   48, 85
  s. 12C(5)   48, 86
  s. 12C(6)   86
  s. 12D   44
  s. 12D(1)   40, 86
  s. 12D(2)   40, 41, 86
  s. 12D(3)–(4)   41, 86
  s. 13   18, 28, 42, 44, 48, 50, 59, 60, 61, 123
  s. 13(1)   4, 86
  s. 13(1)(a)   48, 59
  s. 13(1)(b)   60
  s. 13(2)   86
  s. 14   18, 28, 31, 50, 123, 135
  s. 14(1)   87, 135
  s. 14(2)–(5)   87
  s. 15   18, 28, 123
  s. 15(1)   87–8
  s. 15(2)–(4)   88
  s. 15(5)   88–9
  s. 16   18, 28, 49, 50, 123
  s. 16(1)   49, 50, 89
  s. 16(2)   89

Landlord and Tenant Act 1987 — *continued*
  s. 16(2)(a)   49, 147
  s. 16(2)(b)   50, 147, 148
  s. 16(3)   50, 89
  s. 16(3)(a)   145
  s. 16(3)(b)   146
  s. 16(4)   89
  s. 16(5)   50, 89
  s. 17   18, 28, 50, 51, 123, 148
  s. 17(1)   89–90
  s. 17(2)   90
  s. 17(3)–(4)   50, 90
  s. 17(5)–(6)   90
  s. 17(7)   91
  s. 18   21, 51, 52, 57, 150, 151
  s. 18(1)   91, 150
  s. 18(1)(a)   57
  s. 18(2)   91
  s. 18(2)(b)   150, 151
  s. 18(3)   51, 52, 57, 91–2
  s. 18(3)(a)–(b)   52
  s. 18(4)   51, 52, 92
  s. 18A   104, 106, 118, 120, 122, 124, 126,
    127, 128, 133, 137, 139, 141, 143,
    144
  s. 18A(1)–(2)   92
  s. 18A(3)   31, 92
  s. 18A(4)   92
  s. 19   53, 61, 62
  s. 19(1)   93
  s. 19(2)   93
  s. 19(2)(a)   62
  s. 19(3)   93
  s. 20(1)   14, 31, 93–4, 124
  s. 20(2)–(5)   94
  s. 25(2)   3
  s. 29(1)   3
  s. 29(4)   4
  s. 29(4)(a)   3
  s. 32   97
  s. 47   38
  s. 48   23, 38, 62
  s. 49   23, 38
  s. 52   61
  s. 52A   60, 61
  s. 54   62
  s. 54(1)   23
  s. 56   15
  s. 58   2, 58
  s. 58(1)   94–5
  s. 58(2)–(3)   58, 95
  s. 59(1)–(3)   95
  s. 60(1)   5, 8, 61, 95–6
  Sch. 1   46
    para. 1   97

Landlord and Tenant Act 1987 — *continued*
    para. 2(1)–(2)   97
    para. 2(3)–(4)   46, 97
    para. 3   46
    para. 3(1)   98
    para. 3(2)   46, 98
    para. 4   46
    para. 4(1)   98
    para. 4(2)   98–9
    para. 4(3)   99
    para. 5(1)–(2)   99
    para. 6   99
    para. 7(1)–(4)   100
    para. 8(1)–(2)   100
    para. 9(1)–(3)   101
    para. 10(1)–(2)   102
    Part I   97–9
    Part II   99–102
Law of Property Act 1925
  s. 52   48
  s. 52(2)(c)   48
  s. 61   33
  s. 196   23
Law of Property (Miscellaneous Provisions)
    Act 1989
  s. 2   17, 30
  s. 2(6)   30
Leasehold Reform Act 1967   5, 6
  s. 2   5, 10
  s. 2(1)   5
  s. 2(1)(a)   6
Leasehold Reform, Housing and Urban
    Development Act 1993
    14, 16
  Part I   66
Local Government Act 1985
  Part IV   94
  s. 10   95
Local Government, Planning and Land Act
    1980
  Part XVI   94

Matrimonial Causes Act 1973
  s. 23A   66
  s. 24   66
  s. 24A   66
Matrimonial and Family Proceedings Act
    1984
  s. 17(1)–(2)   66

New Towns Act 1981   94

Rent Act 1977   5, 13, 14, 96
  s. 1   6
  Sch. 10   60

Rent (Agriculture) Act 1976   96
Rentcharges Act 1977   15

Settled Land Act 1925   15, 65

Town and Country Planning Act 1990
    112, 113
Trusts of Land and Appointment of Trustees
    Act 1996   41

Table of Secondary Legislation

Civil Procedure Rules
    61, 62
County Court Rules
    Ord. 43   61
      r. 2   62
      r. 2(2)   62
      r. 17   62

Housing Act 1996 (Consequential
    Amendments) Order 1997
    (SI 1997/64)   60

Lands Tribunal Rules 1996
    (SI 1996/1021)   61

Rent Assessment Committee (England and
    Wales) (Leasehold Valuation Tribunal)
    Regulations 1993 (SI 1993/2408)
    60
    Sch. 1   60

Rent Assessment Committee (England
    and Wales) (Leasehold Valuation
    Tribunal) (Amendment) Regulations
    1996 (SI 1996/2305)   60
Rent Assessment Committee (England and
    Wales) (Leasehold Valuation Tribunal)
    (Amendment) Regulations 1997
    (SI 1997/1854)   60
Rules of the Supreme Court
    Ord. 5(4)(a)   57
    Ord. 18   56
    Ord. 19(5)   56
    Ord. 88   57
    Ord. 97   62
      r. 14   62
      r. 18   62

Tenants' Rights of First Refusal
    (Amendment) Regulations 1996
    (SI 1996/2371)   52

CHAPTER ONE

Application of the Act

1.1 INTRODUCTION

The Landlord and Tenant Act 1987 (LTA 1987) was introduced in response to a widely held perception that tenants of blocks of flats were insufficiently protected from the scourge of bad management. The radical solution of introducing commonhold tenure in England has found favour with everyone but the legislature, and the dilapidated structure of this part of property law is patched up with more shoddy makeshifts than any other area. The 1987 Act itself was preceded by the Committee of Inquiry on the management of such flats which was chaired by E. G. Nugee QC (the 'Nugee Report'). Regrettably the ensuing Bill was both poorly drafted and rushed through Parliament with unseemly haste. Part I of the Act is intended to protect tenants from the adverse effects of changes in the landlord. This is done by giving them the chance to become the landlord when the landlord proposes to sell. This 'right of pre-emption' was as drafted so flawed that it had to be amended immediately in the Housing Act 1988, and after a very bumpy ride in the courts finally it was almost totally re-cast in the Housing Act 1996. This new version of the tenants' right of pre-emption was at first greeted quite favourably, but close examination reveals serious problems with the way it works.

The purpose of the Act is to give certain tenants of blocks of flats the collective right to buy the landlord's interest when the landlord wishes to dispose of it. This purpose is carried out by very complex procedural provisions and backed by criminal sanctions.

1.2 IDENTIFYING HOW THE ACT APPLIES

The following basic checklist identifies the paragraph where each point is discussed:

(a) *Is it premises to which the Act applies?:*

- whole or part of a building (s. 1(2)(a)) (see 1.3);
- two or more qualifying tenants (s. 1(2)(b)) (see 1.3);
- 50 per cent of flats occupied by qualifying tenants (s. 1(2)(c)) (see 1.3);
- not exceeding 50 per cent non-residential use (s. 1(3)) (see 1.5);
- not an exempt landlord (s. 58) (see 5.27).

(b) *Identify the qualifying tenants* (see 1.11):

- not excluded tenancies (s. 3(1));
- not a tenant of more than two flats (s. 3(2), (3)) (see 1.12);
- not a tenant whose landlord is a qualifying tenant (s. 3(4)).

(c) *Identifying the landlord (s. 2)* (see 1.8):

- the immediate landlord of the qualifying tenants, or of the persons entitled to possession subject to a statutory tenancy;
- where any person who is himself a tenant for a term which when granted is for less than seven years or which is terminable by the landlord within its first seven years their landlord is also a landlord (and so on).

(d) *Not an excepted disposal (s. 4)* (see 1.14)

1.3 PREMISES TO WHICH THE ACT APPLIES

The LTA 1987 applies to premises which satisfy the following conditions in s. 1(2):

(a) they consist of the whole or part of a building; and
(b) they contain two or more flats held by qualifying tenants; and
(c) the number of flats held by such tenants exceeds 50 per cent of the total number of flats contained in the premises.

1.3.1 The premises must consist of the whole or part of a building

The 1987 Act does not deal with the problem of defining what is included within a building. This is because the tenants are entitled to buy what the landlord is selling. Some light is thrown on the meaning of 'building' by the judgment of the then Vice-Chancellor Sir Nicholas Browne-Wilkinson in *Denetower Ltd* v *Toop* [1991] 3 All ER 666. He makes it clear that the court will adopt a robust approach in carrying out the purpose of an Act which is 'ill-drafted, complicated and confused'. He looks specifically at the meaning of 'a building'. It may be important to remember that at this point the court was considering the interpretation of a s. 12 notice (used where the landlord has assigned in breach of the tenant's rights of first refusal). However, it would be absurd if the court were to give a different meaning to 'a building' in different parts of the very brief Part I of this Act.

The Vice Chancellor's view is as follows:

> I accept the tenants' second argument. They submit that the word 'building' is not necessarily confined to the bricks and mortar of which the building is constructed. In *St Thomas's Hospital (Governors)* v *Charing Cross Rly Co.* (1861) I John & H 400, 70 ER 802, it was held that section 92 of the Land Clauses Consolidation Act 1845 (which provided that the owner of land being compulsorily acquired could not be required to convey 'a part only of any house, or other building or manufactory') required the purchase not only of the whole house but also of the gardens and appurtenances of the house.
>
> In the present case, it would be to attribute to Parliament an entirely capricious intention if we were to hold that the tenants' right to purchase did not extend to the gardens and other appurtenances of the flats which are expressly or impliedly included in the demises of the flats to the tenants. In my judgment we are not forced to adopt such an unreasonable construction since it is a perfectly legitimate meaning of the word 'building' that it includes the appurtenances of the building.
>
> Denetower submits that there are other provisions in the Act which indicate that in this Act the word 'building' does not include the appurtenances of such building. Under Part III of the 1987 Act tenants can compulsorily acquire the reversion in certain circumstances. Under section 29(1) the court can make an order affecting 'premises to which this Part applies'. The premises to which Part III applies are defined by section 25(2) so far as relevant in the same way as section 1(2) i.e. as premises 'consist[ing] of' a building. Yet, section 29(4)(a) provides expressly as follows:

'(4)   An acquisition order may, if the court thinks fit — (a) include any yard, garden, outhouse or appurtenance belonging to, or usually enjoyed with, the premises specified in the application on which the order is made . . .'

Denetower submits that section 29(4) shows that, apart from its provisions, yards, gardens, outhouses and appurtenances would not be included in the word 'premises'. Whilst admitting the force of this point, in my judgment it is not decisive in construing such an ill-drafted, complicated and confused Act as this. In my judgment, section 29(4) was inserted in Part III out of an abundance of caution. Certainly there is no logical reason why the tenant who acquires under section 12 of the Act should not be entitled to acquire exactly the same property as could be acquired under Part III: yet there is nothing corresponding to section 29(4) in Part I of the 1987 Act.

I therefore reach the conclusion that the purchase notice under section 12 could have required Denetower to transfer not only the two buildings but also any appurtenances of that building.

What then are the appurtenances of the buildings? There can be no doubt that the gardens are included: they are expressly included in the leases of the flats which are part of the buildings. In my judgment the garages are not appurtenances. The tenants enjoy no rights over the garages under or by virtue of their leases of the flats. The garages are held under quite separate leases; not every flatholder has a garage; the freehold of all the garages is not vested in Denetower. In those circumstances it is impossible to hold that the garages are appurtenant to the buildings. Similarly, the tenants of the buildings enjoy no rights over the unused land, nor is such land used in conjunction with the flats: therefore it is not an appurtenance of the building. As to the roadways and paths over which the tenants have either express or prescriptive rights of way, in my judgment they are appurtenances of the building. However, it may well be that a rent assessment committee acting under section 13(1) may reach the conclusion that the appropriate provision should be that the tenants should not acquire the freehold in the land of the roadway and paths, but be granted perpetual rights of way over them.

The question of what appurtenances are included within a building or part of a building is returned to at 4.6.3 when the procedure for enforcing the right of pre-emption is discussed. However, in the straightforward case of the tenants accepting the landlord's offer this question is somewhat academic. The tenants are entitled to purchase what the landlord offers for sale.

1.3.2 The premises must contain two or more flats held by qualifying tenants

The term 'flat' is defined by s. 60(1) as follows:

> 'flat' means a separate set of premises, whether or not on the same floor, which—
> (a) forms part of a building, and
> (b) is divided horizontally from some other part of that building, and
> (c) is constructed or adapted for use for the purposes of a dwelling; ...

This definition owes much to the definition of 'house' in s. 2 of the Leasehold Reform Act 1967. There is, however, a crucial different approach: the overriding question under s. 2 of the 1967 Act is whether the building is a house 'reasonably so called'; under the 1987 Act the definition of a 'flat' must be applied without the assistance of any such over-arching rubric. All the elements of the definition must be satisfied. The precise wording of the definition is peculiar to this Act:

1.3.2.1 A separate set of premises
How separate the premises needs to be remains to be seen. However, circumstances such as six persons, each with a bedroom, sharing a kitchen and lounge, pose a typical problem. By analogy with cases on the Rent Act 1977 it might be expected that each set of premises would contain all the essentials for self-contained living, and the example given here would thus constitute one set of premises only (see 1.3 above where relevant authorities are referred to).

1.3.2.2 Part of a building
Housing Law, A. Arden (ed.), (London: Sweet & Maxwell), para. 2–1886, makes the very telling point that there may well be flats which consist of rooms in more than one building. The flat may, for example, include a room in an adjacent building.

1.3.2.3 Constructed or adapted for use for the purposes of a dwelling
The similar words in the Leasehold Reform Act 1967, s. 2(1), are 'designed or adapted for living in'. In *Tandon* v *Trustees of Spurgeon's Homes* [1992] 1 All ER 1086, at 1094, Lord Roskill thought that these words in the 1967 Act meant the same as 'designed or adapted for occupation as a residence'.

The similar phrase let 'as a separate dwelling' (Rent Act 1977, s. 1; Housing Act 1985, s. 79; Housing Act 1988, s. 1) has been the subject of numerous decisions. Those concerned with whether a particular unit is a dwelling may be of some assistance. In *Metropolitan Properties* v *Barder* [1968] 1 All ER 536, an au pair's bedroom was not a dwelling – the, then, available authorities were considered in that case. Much reliance has been placed on the common-sense test applied in *Curl* v *Angelo* [1948] 2 All ER 189, CA, which categorises a dwelling as being a place where all the major activities of life (listed by the court as sleeping, cooking and feeding) can be carried on. Another useful authority is *Parkins* v *Westminster City Council* [1998] 13 EG 145, in which a bedroom with rights to use common rooms was not itself a separate dwelling.

1.3.2.4 Divided horizontally from some other part of the building

This derives from s. 2(1)(a) of the Leasehold Reform Act 1967. The Act does not require the other part of the building to be of any particular importance – such as a 'material part'. Presumably an attic or basement not included in the demise will suffice, as will a garage (*cf. Parsons* v *Trustees of Henry Smith's Charity* (1974) 230 EG 1887).

The test of whether the premises is 'a flat' is patently meant to be applied to the building as it now is. The test is not whether it was constructed or adapted etc., but whether it is so constructed or adapted now. Given this, the actual use of the premises is irrelevant. If the premises physically as it is now satisfies the three-part test for being a flat then it is still a flat if the actual use is for some non-residential purpose.

1.3.2.5 Qualifying tenants

The various aspects of this are discussed at 1.11.

1.3.3 The number of flats held by qualifying tenants exceeds 50 per cent of the total number of flats in the premises

The application of this will not always be easy. The first step is to identity the premises to be disposed of by the relevant disposal. Next each flat must be identified. Flats do not have to be occupied to be included in the total but they must physically exist. Thus, a floor set aside for future development into flats contains no flats. A floor containing six unlet flats contains six flats. Flats set aside for the landlord's own use, the use of its servants or employees must be counted in this total. A purpose-built flat set aside for another use, e.g., storage of porter's or cleaner's materials, seems to fall within the definition of a flat. However, it may still fall to be included in the definition of premises occupied other than for residential purposes within s. 1(3) (see 1.5). The final step is to calculate the number of flats held by qualifying tenants (see 1.11 below).

1.4 LAND AND OTHER RIGHTS ASSOCIATED WITH BUILDING

The LTA 1987 is very unclear in its operation as regards the issue of how much ancillary land and associated rights are included. The starting point is s. 1(2)(a), which provides that the Act applies to the whole or part of a building. There is no definition of a building (see 1.3.1). Neither is there any direction in the Act as to what ancillary land or rights are to be included in a purchase. The *prima facie* position is that the tenants are entitled to buy whatever the landlord has contracted to sell. It is to be expected that the parcel which the landlord offers for sale will make commercial sense otherwise the landlord would not be able to dispose of it profitably.

There are reported cases where the dispute is about which amenity land or rights over such land the tenants are entitled to acquire. These are dealt with at 4.9 because they concern enforcement by the tenants of their rights against a purchaser from the landlord.

Neither the court not the Lands Tribunal has power to include in a landlord's notice under ss. 5A to 5E (see Appendix B) any property or rights outside the building which are not included by the landlord in that notice. This gives potential scope for avoidance of the Act which is discussed further in chapter 5.

1.5 BUILDINGS WITH A MIXED USE

Under s. 1(3) of the LTA 1987, there is an exception from the Act for premises with a preponderance of non-residential use. The question is whether the internal floor area of the parts occupied or intended to be occupied other than for non-residential purposes exceeds 50 per cent of the whole internal floor area. To apply this exception to a particular transaction there are several steps:

(a) First identify the premises which are being considered. As has been seen, the 1987 Act applies on a building-by-building basis not on a title-by-title basis. Thus, this non-residential use exception cannot be used to evade the Act by simply adding commercial and residential properties within the same title.

(b) Next there must be identified which parts of the premises are occupied or intended to be occupied otherwise than for residential purposes. This concept of 'intended to be occupied' is not explained further in the Act. It could literally refer to an intention existing at the time of building, or it could refer to a present intention. In the context of this Act the latter is the only sensible view. The question is, therefore, whether a particular part of the building in question is occupied otherwise than for residential purposes, or whether it is presently intended to be occupied otherwise than for residential purposes? A further possible ambiguity is the question of whose intention is relevant. The landlord and the tenant might not be as one on this. In modern leases the use clause will be decisive in most cases. If there has been a permitted or tolerated change of use of the relevant part that may determine the issue. There will, however, be some situations where the lease is silent. In these cases, presumably the interior lay-out and structure of an occupied building will be looked at.

(c) The next stage is to calculate the floor area of any internal common parts. There is a definition of 'common parts' in s. 60(1):

> 'common parts', in relation to any building or part of a building, includes the structure and exterior of that building or part and any common facilities within it; . . .

In order to apply this it is necessary to revert to the definition of a 'building' (above, 1.3.1). The crucial part of this definition is that the common facilities must be *within* the building. At first sight, therefore, it would seem that ancillary facilities such as squash courts, swimming pools and gymnasia may be excluded. However, in the result it makes little difference – if these facilities are defined as 'in the building' then they are excluded from the calculation; if they are not 'in the building' they are excluded from the calculation in any event.

(d) The final stage is to see if the floor area (excluding the 'common parts') used for non-residential purposes exceeds 50 per cent of the floor area of the premises. It goes without saying that a solicitor advising on this Act will, unless the application of the provisions is plain and obvious, advise the client to employ a suitable surveyor to make any necessary calculations under s. 1(3).

1.6   LAND HELD UNDER DIFFERENT TITLES

The 1987 Act applies to building and parts of buildings. It does not matter that the building is held under a number of titles. (The landlord may have acquired the property piecemeal so that it is made up of several Land Registry titles.) This issue was the subject of some discussion by the Court of Appeal in *Kay Green* v *Twinsectra Ltd* [1996] 4 All ER 546, at 557. Aldous LJ explained the correct approach:

> I cannot accept the conclusion of the judge that title is relevant. The premises must consist of the whole or part of a building which, as was made clear in *Belvedere*, could include a garden. The word 'premises' does not have a special meaning. It is a word which over the years has been applied to houses, land, shops, and the like with the result that it has come to mean real property of some kind. Thus the 1987 Act states that a landlord should not make a relevant disposal affecting any real property without serving a section 5 notice, if it consists of the whole or part of a building and it contains two or more flats held by qualifying tenants and the number of those flats exceeds 50 per cent of the total. The fact that the building is included within one or more titles is irrelevant. It follows that the question of whether a relevant disposal of premises has been made has to be considered on a building by building basis. Thus when ascertaining whether the applicants were a requisite majority, it is not appropriate to take into account Parr Court. Each building must be considered separately.

Section 5(3) of the Act makes it clear how disposals by the landlord of more than one building are to be handled. This subsection is examined in the next paragraph.

1.7 APPLICATION TO ESTATES INCLUDING MORE THAN ONE BUILDING

Section 5(3) of the LTA 1987 (inserted by Sch. 6 of the Housing Act 1996) attempts to prevent the tenants' right of pre-emption being defeated by the landlord including several properties in the same sale. The precise words are important:

> (3)   Where a landlord proposes to effect a transaction involving the disposal of an estate or interest in more than one building (whether or not involving the same estate or interest), he shall, for the purpose of complying with this section, sever the transaction so as to deal with each building separately.

This possibly does not prevent a 'job lot' of buildings being sold together, provided that the consideration is severed to so as to be attributable to each building and provided that a separate offer notice is served on each building's tenants.

So far as auction sales are concerned, there is no obviously sensible route for compliance other than by offering each building as a separate lot. A case may conceivably arise where a seller might think it worthwhile to offer a collection of properties in an auction as one lot but specifying a fractional apportionment of the price between each building. The auction contract will also have to provide for the winner of the auction to accept that individual buildings may succumb to the tenants' right of pre-emption (see further 2.6).

A more robust construction of s. 5(3) would give the expression 'sever' the meaning that there must actually be separate contracts for each building, but this is somewhat academic in practice. The effect of severance is intended to be that the tenants of each building will be able to accept an offer in respect of their own part.

The tenants in question may, of course, actually prefer to purchase all the buildings on an estate. Landlords who communicate effectively with tenants will be in a better position to manage such dispositions.

It is suggested in *Woodfall, Landlord and Tenant* (London: Sweet & Maxwell), para. L28.007, that 'it is probable, however, that the definition should be read as if it covered premises consisting of the whole or part of a building or building scheme'. Here, the definition *Woodfall* refers to is the definition of a building. The case of *30 Upperton Gardens Management* v *Akano* [1990] 2 EGLR 232, is cited in support of this. *Akano* is only a leasehold valuation tribunal decision. It is concerned with the LTA 1987 before its amendment by the Housing Act 1996. It is also concerned with a case where there had been a transfer not complying with the Act. Given the now clear wording of s. 5(3), *Akano* cannot be regarded as a useful authority on this point. Thus, where there is a number of buildings on a building scheme, the better view is that severance on a building-by-building basis must take place.

A solicitor preparing notices may find it necessary to have the opinion of a surveyor on whether particular structures constitute one building or are separate buildings. It can be expected that the court will take a common-sense approach akin to the decision whether property is a 'house' within the Leasehold Reform Act 1967, s. 2 (see e.g., *Malpas* v *St. Ermin's Property Co. Ltd* (1992) 24 HLR 537). The question is, would someone looking at it say that this is a separate building?

'Building' must mean a building with tenants in. Separate structures such as squash courts, garage blocks and so on are not buildings for the purpose of severance under s. 5(3). This must be so or the 1987 Act would be a complete nonsense.

1.8 LANDLORD

The landlord is generally the immediate reversioner to the qualifying tenants (s. 2(1)(a)). If there is a statutory tenant then the landlord is the person who would be entitled to possession if there were no statutory tenancy (see s. 2(1)(b)).

If the immediate landlord is itself a tenant under a tenancy for a term of less than seven years or a term terminable within the first seven years then its landlord is also a landlord under the 1987 Act. This can be repeated *ad infinitum* until a landlord is found with a tenancy of more than seven years.

This definition means that if there are any leases superior to the qualifying tenants' leases, which include a number (or all) of the flats then the freehold (or superior lease, which is superior to the lease out of which the qualifying tenants are created) can be sold without there being a disposal within the 1987 Act. The following paragraph develops this point.

1.9 SUB-TENANCY SITUATIONS

Many blocks of flats have complex tenancy structures. Some are arrangements made to facilitate the business structures of the landlord; some are to assist in the enforceability of covenants and the collection of service charges. Many complexities arise by chance over the passage of time. Typical situations are as follows:

(a) The freehold is subject to a long lease under which the flat owners all hold with each having an individual sub-lease. In this case the sale of the freehold as such is not within the LTA 1987, Part I, because the freeholder has no qualifying tenants.

(b) The property is let by the freeholder on long leases of each flat, some of which are subject to short sub-tenancies. In this case each long leaseholder may be a qualifying tenant. The tenants who hold the short sub-tenancies will not be qualifying tenants if their head tenant is a qualifying tenant (s. 3(4)).

In the rough and tumble of practice, with the passage of time sub-tenancy structures become elaborate and even opaque. Some possible scenarios are as follows:

(a) Where below the freehold there are mesne long tenancies of the whole. In this case only a disposal of the leases immediately superior to a qualifying lease will trigger the operation of the Act (see *Belvedere Court Management Ltd* v *Frogmore Developments Ltd* [1996] 1 All ER 312).

(b) Where below the freehold there are mesne tenancies of part of the building. Attlee House has 100 flats. The freeholder (F) lets 30 flats on a 99-year lease to X and 70 flats on a 99-year lease to Y. Each of the 100 flats is then underlet to a tenant in possession. Assume that each tenant in possession satisfies the definition of a qualifying tenant in s. 3 of the 1987 Act (see 1.11). In respect of their relevant tenancies then, X and Y are the landlords. A disposal by F of his interest does not trigger the Act. However, a disposal by either X or Y clearly does trigger the operation of the Act, because it applies to disposals of the whole or of part of a building (s. 1(2)(a)).

1.10   APPLICATION TO SUB-SALES

A sub-sale may be a disposal under the 1987 Act unless it falls within s. 4(2)(i) which deals with disposals in pursuance of a contract (see 1.17). A sub-sale may occur in a number of ways:

(a) Having entered into a contract the purchaser may then contract to sell the land to a sub-purchaser. This sub-contract will be a disposal in itself within s. 4A(2)(a).

(b) Having entered into a contract the purchaser may then assign the benefit of the contract to an assignee. This will be a disposal under s. 4A(2)(b).

(c) Having entered into a contract to purchase the land the purchaser may simply direct the seller to transfer the land to a nominee. This transfer will not be itself a disposal. It will fall within the exception in s. 4(2)(i) as 'a disposal in pursuance of a contract'.

1.11   QUALIFYING TENANT

Provided that the unit in question is a flat, a tenant is a qualifying tenant unless one of the exceptions in s. 3 of the LTA 1987 applies. These exceptions are as follows:

1.11.1   A protected shorthold tenancy under the Housing Act 1980, s. 52

These tenancies were the direct ancestor of the present assured shorthold tenancy. The relevant part of the Housing Act 1988 came into force on 28 November 1988 and no new protected shorthold tenancies can be created after 14 January 1989 (Housing Act 1988, s. 34) except in the rare cases provided for by s. 34 itself.

1.11.2 Business tenancies

A 'business tenancy' is a tenancy under the Landlord and Tenant Act 1954, Part II. If the tenancy is of or includes premises occupied by the tenant for the purposes of a business then the tenancy falls within the 1954 Act.

1.11.3 A tenancy terminable on the cessation of the tenant's employment

Most examples of service occupancy will not be tenancies at all. This was reclarified by Lord Templeman in *Street* v *Mountford* [1988] AC 809. There will be no tenancy where the occupation is necessary for the employee to perform his work; the employee is required to occupy the premises for those purposes; and the occupation is ancillary to the performance of the employee's duty (this test derives from *Smith* v *Seghill Overseers* (1875) LR 10 QB 422). It can be seen from this definition that there may be a tenancy terminable on the cessation of employment, i.e., a tenancy which has a term requiring termination on cessation of employment but which does not satisfy the strict test reiterated in *Street* v *Mountford*.

1.11.4 An assured tenancy or assured agricultural occupancy

From 15 January 1989 (commencement of relevant parts of the Housing Act 1988) most residential tenancies are assured tenancies. Note, however, that:

(a) Rent Act tenancies (which will still exist for many years) are not excepted from the 1987 Act. A regulated tenancy will thus be a qualifying tenancy unless the tenant's landlord is a qualifying tenant (see LTA 1987, s. 3(4));

(b) new Rent Act tenancies created under the transitional provisions (s. 34) of the Housing Act 1988 are not excepted from the 1987 Act. These are:

    (i)   tenancies granted under a contract made before 15 January 1989 which would otherwise have fallen within the Rent Act 1977,

    (ii) tenancies granted after 14 January 1989 to an existing Rent Act tenant by his landlord or one of his joint landlords,

(iii) in some cases a landlord may obtain possession of a Rent Act 1977 tenancy on the ground that suitable alternative accommodation is available. The court may direct that the new tenancy will be a Rent Act 1977 tenancy (Housing Act 1988, s. 34(1)(c)). The court must have 'considered that, in the circumstances, the grant of an assured tenancy would not afford the required security'.

1.12 MULTIPLE FLAT HOLDERS

A person cannot be a qualifying tenant if he holds three flats in the same premises (LTA 1987, s. 3(2)). For this purpose flats which fall under excepted tenancies (see. 1.11) are not counted. However, flats which are held by an associated company and which are not in themselves excepted tenancies are counted (s. 3(3)). An associated company is a company's holding company, or subsidiary or a fellow subsidiary of the same holding company (see s. 736 of the Companies Act 1985: LTA 1987, s. 20(1)).

1.13 RELEVANT DISPOSALS

The 1987 Act is designed to apply to any disposal by the landlord. The words used are sweeping: 'the disposal by the landlord of any estate or interest (whether legal or equitable) in any such premises, including the disposal of any such estate or interest in any common parts of any such premises ...' (LTA 1987, s. 4(1)). However, this apparently all-embracing rubric is followed by a daunting list of exceptional cases (see 1.14). This list, because of the scope it gave for avoidance, was amended by the 1988 and 1996 Housing Acts and also by the Leasehold Reform Housing and Urban Development Act 1993.

The Court decided, somewhat oddly, in *Mainwaring v Trustees of Henry Smith's Charity* (1996) 28 HLR 584, CA, that 'disposal' did not include a contract to dispose of the premises. This lacuna in the 1987 Act was removed by the insertion of a new s. 4A by s. 89 of the Housing Act 1996 (see below). The same case decided that if the disposal is by a transfer of registered land, the date of the disposal is the execution of the transfer in unconditional form, rather than the actual registration of the transfer. On this point *Mainwaring* is unaffected by the Housing Act 1996.

A disposal of part of the estate over which the tenant has legal rights must be a disposal within the Act. Thus, if the tenants have in their lease rights to use garden land the landlord cannot dispose of the garden land, without complying with the Act (see 1.3).

1.14 EXCEPTED DISPOSALS

1.14.1 Disposal of a single flat

The grant of a tenancy of a single flat (whether with or without its appurtenant premises) is not a relevant disposal (LTA 1987, s. 4(1)(a)). This seems to include a disposition which is a reversionary lease.

1.14.2 Disposals of certain interests

Certain interests in land can be disposed of without there being a relevant disposal. These are:

(a) the interest of a Settled Land Act beneficiary;
(b) incorporeal hereditaments – for practical purposes this now means rentcharges; easements; profits à prendre and franchises (LTA 1987, s. 4(2)(a)(iii)). Rentcharges can now be created only in the circumstances permitted by the Rentcharges Act 1977. For practical purposes this means estate rentcharges (i.e. those used to assist in the enforcement of positive covenants or the collection of service charges). Franchises can be granted only by the Crown, and because of the limited application of the 1987 Act to Crown land (s. 56) are of no significance.

There is an academic argument that reversions and remainders are incorporeal hereditaments. That this is an error is clearly shown by Megarry and Wade in *The Law of Real Property*, 4th ed. (London: Stevens, 1975), p. 790, and a full explanation of how the error arose is found in *Challis's Real Property*, 3rd ed. (London: Butterworths, 1911), pp. 48–58. This lengthy historical note by Charles Sweet demonstrates how Challis had fallen into error by resting his classification of different land law interests upon the technicalities of conveyancing rather than the nature of the interests. It is clear beyond any doubt that in this Act incorporeal heriditaments do not include reversions or the Act would be completely futile;
(c) securities (LTA 1987, s. 4(2)(aa)). This is a 'disposal ... by way of security for a loan'. This gives at first sight a modest scope for avoidance of the Act. However, s. 4(1A) (added by the Housing Act 1988, Sch. 13) makes it clear that a disposal by a mortgagee in exercise of a power of sale or leasing is not an excepted disposal.

1.14.3 'Involuntary' disposals

These are disposals to trustees in bankruptcy or the liquidator of a company; disposals under a court order or under s. 2 of the Inheritance

(Provision for Family and Dependants) Act 1975; disposals under compulsory purchase orders or agreements in lieu of compulsory purchase orders and disposals under the Leasehold Reform, Housing and Urban Development Act 1993 (LTA 1987, s. 4(2)(b)–(da)).

1.14.4 Certain conveyances at 'undervalue'

These are gifts to family or to charity; disposals by one charity to another of functional land; disposals on the appointment or discharge of a trustee; disposals between members of a family and a disposal under a will or on intestacy (LTA 1987, s. 4(2)(e)–(h) and (3)(b)).

There is a definition of 'family' in s. 4(5):

> (5)   A person is a member of another's family for the purposes of this section if—
>   (a)   that person is the spouse of that other person, or the two of them live together as husband and wife, or
>   (b)   that person is that other person's parent, grandparent, child, grandchild, brother, sister, uncle, aunt, nephew or niece.

Section 4(6) states that for the purposes of s. 4(5)(b) a relationship by marriage shall be treated as a relationship by blood and a relationship of the half-blood shall be treated as a relationship of the whole blood, the stepchild of a person shall be treated as his child, and an illegitimate child shall be treated as the legitimate child of his mother and reputed father.

It will be noted that there is no requirement that couples should be married couples provided that they are living together as husband and wife. This excludes couples of the same sex, (see, e.g., *Harrogate BC* v *Simpson* (1984) 17 HLR 205; *Fitzpatrick* v *Sterling Housing Associations Ltd* [1997] 4 All ER 991, which contains a very helpful discussion of a similar statutory provision).

1.14.5 Certain miscellaneous transactions

The following disposals are also not 'relevant' disposals for the purposes of Part I of the LTA 1987:

(a)   a surrender of a tenancy pursuant to a term of that tenancy (s. 4(2)(j));
(b)   a disposal to the Crown (s. 4(2)(k));
(c)   a disposal pursuant to any option or right of pre-emption (see 1.15: s. 4(2)(i)(i)).

(d) a disposal pursuant to any obligation created before 1 February 1988 (the commencement of the Act: s. 4(2)(i)(ii)).

1.14.6 Associated company disposals

The definition of an 'associated company' has already been considered (see 1.12). Property holding companies found associated companies a very good way of avoiding the 1987 Act. Property that they intended to dispose of would simply be transferred to an associated company. This associated company could then be disposed of by a sale of its shares, this clearly not involving a disposal under the Act. To counteract this s. 4(2)(l) was amended so as to apply only to an associate company which has been an associated company for at least two years. This makes the use of associated company schemes more difficult but by no means impossible (see further chapter 5).

1.15 APPLICATION TO CONTRACTS AND OPTIONS

As originally drafted the application of the Act to contracts was unclear. The unsatisfactory position was explored by the Court of Appeal in *Mainwaring* v *Trustees of Henry Smith's Charity* (1996) 28 HLR 584. As a result a new s. 4A and amended s. 4(2)(i) were inserted into the 1987 Act by s. 89 of the Housing Act 1996.

1.15.1 Contracts affected

All contracts are disposals. Section 4A(1) of the LTA 1987 applies to conditional and unconditional contracts. It applies whether or not the contract is enforceable by specific performance. A contract which does not comply with the requirement for writing under s. 2 of the Law of Property (Miscellaneous Provisions) Act 1989 is not a contract and accordingly not a disposition within the 1987 Act. If the legal estate is disposed of apparently pursuant to the contract then the procedure laid down by the new s. 5 (offer notice: requirements in case of conveyance not preceded by contract, etc.) must be complied with. There has been some confusion in practice as to the effect of this provision. If a conditional contract is entered into a s. 5 notice must first have been served or the landlord will be guilty of a criminal offence (see chapter 5). This means that conditional contracts have very limited use as a means of avoiding the Act.

1.15.2 Disposal in pursuance of option or right of pre-emption

A disposal pursuant to an option or right of pre-emption is dealt with by the LTA 1987, s. 8D. Sections 11 to 17 take effect as if the disposal pursuant to the option were the relevant disposal.

This applies only if the second disposal is within four months of whichever is the earlier of:

(a) notices under s. 3A of the Landlord and Tenant Act 1985 being served on the requisite majority of qualifying tenants; or

(b) other documents being served on them which tell them of the original disposal and alert them to their rights and the time in which they should be exercised.

If a disposal pursuant to an option or right of pre-emption takes place outside this four-month period then it is exempt under s. 4(2)(i).

1.15.3 How s. 8D works

Section 8D applies where there is an original disposal which is the grant of an option or a right of pre-emption. By virtue of s. 11, if the Act is not complied with the tenants have rights against the purchaser. If there is a disposal in exercise of that grant which is made within the four-month period described in s. 8D(2) then s. 11 applies as if that disposal in exercise of the grant is the original disposal. The tenants then have in respect of that exercise the rights given by s. 11A *et seq.*

If a s. 5 notice is served before the original grant then the disposal in exercise of the grant is exempt. It has to be said that s. 8D could be read as if it applied even where a s. 5 notice was served at the time of the original grant. However, this would be to read s. 8D out of context. Its purpose is to tailor the s. 11A procedure and the following sections to cases where a grant has been followed by the exercise of the grant. These sections of course apply only where the s. 8 procedure is not followed.

1.15.4 Summary of Act's application to options and rights of pre-emption

(a) The grant of an option or right of pre-emption (but see 2.8) is a relevant disposal (LTA 1987, s. 4(1)).

(b) The assignment of an option contract or right of pre-emption (but see 2.8) may be a relevant disposal (s. 4A(2)) if made by the landlord.

(c) A disposal in pursuance of an option or right of pre-emption is exempt unless s. 8D of the 1987 Act applies (see 1.18).

(d) Section 8D applies to a disposal exercise of an option or right of pre-emption comes within s. 8D if it is made within four months of the tenants having written notice of the original disposal having taken place (see 1.18 for discussion of this very badly worded section).

CHAPTER TWO

The Offer Notices

2.1 THE OFFER NOTICE

A landlord must not effect a relevant disposal unless the correct offer notice has been served on the qualifying tenants (LTA 1987, s. 5). The properties in respect of which a notice must be served are referred to as 'the constituent flats'. There are different offer notices dealing with different types of potential disposals (s. 5(2): see 2.5–2.9 below).

2.2 DISPOSAL OF SEVERAL BUILDINGS

If the landlord wishes to dispose of several buildings together – say to another property holding company – then this can be accomplished. First, though, a separate offer notice must be served on the tenants of each building. This effectively means that there must be a separate consideration shown for each building. If any part of the consideration is not money then a s. 5E offer notice must be used (see 2.9).

The practical difficulties of disposing of a site involving several buildings are considerable. Section 5(3) of the 1987 Act makes it clear that for an effective offer notice the landlord 'shall' for the purposes of complying with this section, sever the transaction or deal with each building separately. In practical terms the following points may be considered:

(a) A determination must be made as to what is 'each building' on the site. There will be many scenarios when a solicitor will feel the need for expert assistance from a surveyor in arriving at a view on this.

(b) A s. 5 notice must be served which deals with each building separately. This must mean that the tenants of each building are given a separate opportunity to purchase their building. It does not seem to prevent them also being given the opportunity to purchase the whole. Thus, suppose a site consists of 12 blocks of flats on one estate. The landlord might be advised that an obtainable market price for its interest in the whole is £200,000. There is no reason why each block cannot be valued at £16,666 and the entire common parts, tennis court, garages and other areas at £8.00. A purchaser in a proposed disposal might have the chance to purchase the entire estate only, but the tenants might be given the opportunity to purchase either their separate building or the whole estate. Doubtless the draftperson's ingenuity can achieve both severance and a package that makes purchase as a whole the only sensible option.

(c) The s. 18 procedure (see 4.12) may possibly be used.

(d) It may be felt that the difficulties caused by the need to comply with s. 5(3) are insuperable. Coming to an understanding with the tenants – especially where there are established tenants' groups – may be a way out of this problem. It becomes a matter of commercial judgment whether the clarity of understanding with the tenants allows procedures under the Act to be curtailed. Many will feel that even the remote risk of prosecution (see chapter 5) cannot be ignored.

(e) If a disposal of part does take place then problems may be caused with severance of the service charge and with the leasehold title. These are as follows:

   (i) *Severance of buildings – service charge problems.* Where there is a number of buildings in an estate scheme then severance pursuant to s. 5(3) may be practically difficult. Suppose there are ten buildings of ten flats each paying 1 per cent of the service charge amount. If one building is sold then there is a perceived problem with shared services. The tenants' leases will ordinarily entitle them to go on using the shared services and the service charge fraction will remain correct. The problem is less a legal one than a practical and commercial problem. Property companies are reluctant to continue to administer service charge schemes for parts of the estate which are owned by the tenants. From the landlord's perspective there is no one obvious solution to the practical problem. There is no difficulty if a sale of all ten buildings to the tenants can be negotiated. There is some possibility of structuring the offer for sale so that it is disadvantageous to buy a single building without buying the whole estate. It would clearly be more sensible if the Act were amended to allow the landlord to deal with estate schemes including several buildings without the need for severance on a building-by-building basis.

(ii)   *Severance of buildings – title problems.* The most obvious title problem arises where the landlord's interest is a leasehold which contains an absolute prohibition on assignment of part. In this case the dictates of s. 5(3), requiring severance on a building-by-building basis, cannot be followed. If the covenant is a qualified covenant then the provisions of s. 8E (introduced by the Housing Act 1996) become relevant. These are discussed below at 3.7.

(f)   Where the landlord wishes to sell as a whole but is forced to sever to comply with s. 5(3) then consideration has to be given to what grants, reservations and possibly covenants are included in the sale of each part. This gives considerable scope for putting pressure upon the tenants to buy the whole of an estate and not see it break up into parts. There is nothing in the Act which allows the leasehold valuation tribunal or the court to re-write the terms of the proposed disposal or, it would also seem, the terms of the severance which is made in order to comply with s. 5(3).

2.3   SERVICE OF THE OFFER NOTICE

In order to satisfy s. 5 of the 1987 Act, the landlord must succeed in serving the offer notice on at least 90 per cent of the qualifying tenants, or, if there are less than ten, on all but one of them (LTA 1987, s. 5(5)). The question may sometimes arise whether a landlord can deliberately choose not to serve a notice on some small number of the tenants, whether because they may be harder to serve or for some other reason. If this course of action is adopted there may be a risk of prosecution for a criminal offence under s. 10A of the Act (this is dealt with at chapter 5).

The Interpretation Act 1978, s. 7, applies to service by post:

Where an Act authorises or requires any document to be served by post (whether the expression 'serve' or the expression 'give' or 'send' or any other expression is used), then, unless the contrary intention appears, the service is deemed to be effected by properly addressing, pre-paying and posting a letter containing the document and, unless the contrary is proved, to have been effected at the time at which the letter would be delivered in the ordinary course of post.

This provision was applied in the very illuminating case of *Chiswell* v *Griffon Land and Estates* [1975] 2 All ER 665, a case concerning service by a tenant of notice that he did not wish to give up a business tenancy. There was evidence given by the tenant's solicitor that the letter giving such notice was posted, and the court believed this. There was evidence given by the landlord's solicitor that the letter was not received, and the court believed this. This meant that in the result the presumption of service found in the statute was rebutted. The evidence needed to rebut the presumption is only 'on the balance of probabilities'. The Court of Appeal was unanimous and firm in rejecting any higher standard.

2.4   METHOD OF SERVICE OF NOTICES

Section 54(1) of the LTA 1987 provides that notices under the Act must be in writing and may be served by post. Section 196 of the Law of Property Act 1925 ('Regulations respecting notices') does not apply to notices served under the 1987 Act. The reference in s. 49 of the LTA 1987 may mislead on this point – it extends service under s. 196 of the 1925 Act to the statutory addresses furnished under s. 48 of the 1987 Act, but it does not as such apply s. 196 to statutory notices under Part I of the 1987 Act. The result is as follows:

(a) *Landlord's service.* The landlord may serve the offer notice by personal service on the tenant or by post. This makes the practical decision as to service one to which some thought must be given. The use of recorded delivery will clearly make it very unlikely that a tenant can rebut the presumption that service has been effected.

(b) *Time of service.* It may be necessary to calculate the precise day of service of a landlord's notice. For calculating all the periods which depend on the date of service, the relevant date is the date on which the last qualifying tenant was actually served (LTA 1987, s. 5(4)).

2.5 SECTION 5A OFFER NOTICE: WHERE DISPOSAL IS A CONTRACT TO CREATE OR TRANSFER AN ESTATE OR INTEREST IN LAND

A precedent for an offer notice is set out at Appendix B. There is no prescribed form to be used. The content of the notice must simply comply with s. 5A.

Section 5A(2) requires the notice to contain the principal terms of the proposed contract, including the description of the property, the deposit and consideration. Since a sale cannot be made on different terms (see 3.5) much care must be given to drafting this. The most straightforward way to achieve accuracy is by attaching the proposed contract itself to the offer notice.

Under s. 5A(3) the notice must contain a formal statement that it is an offer notice capable of being accepted by the requisite majority of tenants.

Under s. 5A(4) the notice has to specify a period of time of at least two months from service of the offer notice within which the offer can be accepted. There is no maximum period which can be specified. Effectively the two-month period runs from the date of service on the last qualifying tenant to be served. Under s. 5A(5) the notice must specify a further period of at least two months within which the tenants may nominate who the purchaser will be, 'the nominated person'. The landlord may specify a period of any length so long as it is at least two months.

Doubt has been expressed whether this further period of two months must run from the end of the two-month period in s. 5A(4), or whether it can run from when the offer is accepted. The logical answer is that that the further two months should run from the acceptance notice since its purpose is to provide a 'protected period' after the acceptance notice (see 3.1) during which no disposal by the landlord can be made. The definition in s. 6(4) of the LTA 1987 of the 'protected' period as being a period beginning with the date of service of the acceptance notice is some (but not especially strong) support for the view that the further two-month period may be expressed as starting from the service of the acceptance notice. The statutory provision is, nevertheless, ambiguous and *ex abundantia cautela* the landlord may wish to serve a notice which allows two months (at least) from the end of the period of two months allowed for the acceptance notice.

Under s. 5A(6), s. 5A does not apply to grants of options or rights of pre-emption. These are dealt with by s. 5C (see 2.7).

2.6 SECTION 5B OFFER NOTICE IN CASES OF SALE BY AUCTION

The procedure under s. 5B of the LTA 1987 is particularly complicated. It applies to a sale at a public auction. The expression 'public auction' is not defined. The Romans (23 Livy 37) had a formal way of indicating the existence of a public auction – by the planting of a spear in the ground (but see Zuleta, *The Roman Law of Sale*, p. 56, n. 7, which suggests that this may not be a legal incident of an auction). In English law the matter is bereft of analysis and the expression probably simply means an auction 'open to all'. The question may one day arise what is the procedure to be adopted where the sale is by a non-public auction, e.g., where selected persons are invited to bid. The framework of the 1987 Act dictates that such a disposal must come within one of ss. 5A to 5E. The disposal is definitely a relevant disposal and s. 5 provides that a landlord who proposes to make a relevant disposal 'shall serve a notice under this section'; and s. 5(1) that the notice must comply with the requirements of whichever of the following sections is applicable. Regrettably none applies to a non-public auction and the probable conclusion is that such a mode of sale cannot be held in compliance with the 1987 Act.

Where a sale is required to be by public auction then it undoubtedly does not include a sale by private treaty 'in the room'. Thus if a s. 5B notice has been given, a disposal by private treaty 'in the room' will be a breach of the Act giving rise to Criminal penalties (see chapter 5). Similarly a sale under s. 6 by a further public auction is not satisfied if the eventual disposal is a private treaty however arrived at. (These points are raised in [1998] 21 EG 154, but it is felt the clear answer given here is correct.)

The s. 5B notice must meet the following requirements:

(a) it must state the principal terms of the sale (s. 5B(2));
(b) it must state that the sale is to be made by public auction (s. 5B(3));
(c) it must state that the landlord's offer is for the tenants to take over the purchase after the auction (s. 5B(4));
(d) it must specify a period (of at least two months) from service for the tenants to accept the offer (s. 5B(5));
(e) it must specify a further period of at least 28 days for a nominated person to be selected by the tenants (s. 5B(6)).

Section deals with the timescale for the various procedures (see Table 2.1). Section 5B(8) requires the landlord to serve notice of the time and place of the auction unless this is contained in the offer notice.

(See 2.5 above for comment on equivalent provisions for s. 5A notices).

Table 2.1   Timescale for sales by public auction

Time	Procedure
4 to 6 months before auction	serve offer notice
at least 2 months before auction	end of acceptance period
at least 28 days before auction	end of period for nominating purchaser
at least 28 days before auction	serve details of time and place of auctions (unless in offer notice).

2.7   SECTION 5C OFFER NOTICE: GRANT OF AN OPTION OR RIGHT OF PRE-EMPTION

Section 5C of the LTA 1987 applies to both options and rights of pre-emption, though the application of the Act to rights of pre-emption is not entirely clear.

It is basic law that the grant of a right of pre-emption is not the grant of an interest in land (see, e.g., the analysis by Goff LJ (as he then was) in *Pritchard* v *Briggs* [1980] 1 All ER 294). Accordingly the grant of a right of pre-emption is not on the face of things capable of being a relevant disposal with s. 4(1) of the 1987 Act, nor is a contract to grant a right of pre-emption capable of falling within s. 4A. However, a disposal pursuant to 'a contract, option or right of pre-emption' is exempt under s. 4(2). The literal effect of this would be that neither a grant of a right of pre-emption nor a disposal pursuant to a right of pre-emption would fall within the scheme of the Act. Yet it is perfectly clear from the inclusion of rights of pre-emption within s. 5C that they are intended to be included in the Act and to be treated in the same way as options. The draftsperson must thus have (incorrectly) assumed that the grant of a right of pre-emption was the grant of an interest in land. It can be assumed that the court will 'apply a strained construction in order to tailor the enactment to the true legal rule' (Bennion, *Statutory Interpretation*, Butterworths, 1984, p. 344 – giving as examples of this process *Land Securities plc* v *Receiver for the Metropolitan Police District* [1983] 2 All ER 254; *R* v *Lincoln (Kesteven) Justices, ex parte O'Connor* [1983] Crim LR 621; *Box Parish Council* v *Lacey* [1979] 1 All ER 113), although in the instant case both the error and the correct reading may be too obvious for the court to need much persuasion.

The format of a s. 5C offer notice follows the same pattern *mutatis mutandis* as those already discussed:

(a) Under s. 5C(3) the notice must state that it is an offer notice offering to grant an option or right of pre-emption which may be accepted by the requisite majority of qualifying tenants. The group of tenants who purchase the option or right of pre-emption may be a very different group from those who are tenants when the events occur which trigger the operation of the right. The commercial nature of options and rights of pre-emption is not suitable to a situation where a shifting population of tenants will be the effective grantee. It is doubtful if the s. 5C procedure will find much use in practice.

(b) Section 5C(4) and (5) lay down similar timescales as are specified for a s. 5A notice (for comment, see 2.5 above).

(c) Section 5C(2) requires the notice to contain the principal terms of the disposal, including the consideration and the principal terms on which the option or right is exercisable.

The case of disposals in pursuance of an option or right of pre-emption is dealt with further at 1.15 above.

The concept of telling the tenants the principal terms on which an offer they may accept is exercisable is a very odd one. A person purchasing an option will naturally wish to know all the terms of the disposal and all the terms on which the right is exercisable. It cannot but be thought that the word 'principal' is carelessly used by the draftsperson throughout s. 5. If it is has any meaning it must mean 'all', or at the least 'all of any significance whatsoever'. It makes no sense for the drafter of an offer notice to gamble on any particular precision of meaning being given to the courts by the word 'principal'. In order to draft offer notices which one can be confident will comply with the Act it is more sensible to include all the terms of the proposed disposal contract. This can conveniently be done by attaching the proposed contract to the offer notice.

2.8 SECTION 5D OFFER NOTICE: CASES WHERE CONVEYANCE NOT PRECEDED BY CONTRACT

It is easy to lose sight of the fact that the two-stage (contract and conveyance) process in conveyancing is nothing other than a more or less convenient custom of the profession.

The offer notice to be used where the disposal is not preceded by a contract follows the same form as the s. 5C offer notice. The form set out at Appendix B can be used for this purpose.

2.9 SECTION 5E OFFER NOTICE: WHERE THERE IS A DISPOSAL FOR NON-MONETARY CONSIDERATION

This offer notice (see Appendix B) must comply with whichever of ss. 5A to 5D is applicable. It must the state that the tenants may make an election under s. 8C. The timescales for tenants to assert their rights under s. 8C are shorter than under other provisions (see 2.9.1) and must be carefully noted. The consideration payable by the tenants which is non-monetary consideration is treated as 'such amount in money as was equivalent to its value in the hands of the landlord' (LTA 1987, s. 8C(4)). Either the landlord or the nominated person may apply to have this figure determined by a leasehold valuation tribunal (s. 8C(4); see chapter 6 for procedures).

2.9.1 Section 8C election

If tenants serve an acceptance notice in respect of an offer notice which falls within s. 5E (disposal for non-monetary consideration) then they may make an election under s. 8C of the Act within the period for serving notice of a nominated person. The tenants having served such a notice are able to proceed under ss. 11–17 against any person to whom the landlord disposes of the property, except that:

(a) under s. 11(A)(3) the four-month period for requesting information is reduced to 28 days;

(b) under s. 12A(2) and s. 12B(3) the period for exercise of tenants' rights against the 'purchaser' is reduced from six months to two months (see s. 8C(3)).

CHAPTER THREE

Further Procedures

3.1 ACCEPTANCE OF LANDLORD'S OFFER

3.1.1 Protected period

The LTA 1987, s. 6(1) provides that once an offer notice has been served the landlord shall not dispose of the protected interest until the period for accepting the offer has expired, or until such longer period as may be agreed with the majority of qualifying tenants has expired. A disposal in contravention of this prohibition is not invalidated (s. 10A(5)). The sanction is that the Landlord may be guilty of a criminal offence under s. 10A.

The point may be made at this stage – though it is of general importance under the Act – that a tenant or tenants may apply to the court for an injunction to prevent a breach by the landlord of its obligations under the Act. The basis of the jurisdiction to award an injunction is clearly explained by Farwell J in *Stevens v Chown* [1901] 1 Ch 894, at 905. He states the pertinent principle as follows:

> Now, if I find that the statute enacts, either by way of new creation or by way of restatement of an ancient right, a right of property, that at once gives rise to the jurisdiction of the Court to protect that right. If the Act goes on to provide a particular remedy for the infringement of that right of property so created, that does not exclude the jurisdiction of this court to protect the right of property, unless the Act in terms says so.

The qualifying tenants and each of them are undoubtedly given property rights by the 1987 Act and can maintain an action for an injunction to restrain these rights being flouted by the landlord.

3.1.2 Extension of protected period

Once a s. 5 offer notice has been served, the landlord cannot dispose of the property during the period it has specified in the notice for accepting the offer except to a person nominated by the requisite majority of the tenants (LTA 1987, s. 6(1)). This period may be extended as much as is wished by agreement between the landlord and the requisite majority of tenants (s. 6(1)(b)).

The remainder of s. 6 deals with the mechanics of acceptance and prevention of the landlord disposing of the property while these procedures are pending.

3.1.3 The s. 6 procedures

Section 6(2) provides that where an acceptance notice has been duly served on the landlord, during the remainder of the 'protected period' (for definition see below) the landlord may dispose of the relevant property only to a person nominated by the qualifying tenants in accordance with the Act.

Section 6(3) provides for the content and service of an acceptance notice. The tenants may or may not accept in full the offer made by the landlord.

An acceptance notice must be served by the requisite majority of tenants of the constituent flats in the period for service stated in the offer notice. Strict compliance with the statutory timescale is required. The court has no power to relieve for failure to meet this timescale. The landlord and tenants may, however, agree a longer period (s. 6(3)(b)). Sensibly any such agreement should be unambiguous and in writing. However, the Act contains no requirement for writing. Neither would the agreement itself be one to which the Law of Property (Miscellaneous Provisions) Act 1989, s. 2 applies. Despite the plethora of cases on s. 2, there is none directly on this point. It is, nevertheless, clear that an agreement to extend the period for service of a statutory notice is not itself an agreement for the disposition of an interest in land within s. 2(6) of that Act.

The 'protected period' is defined by s. 6(4). In order to calculate this, the starting date is the date of service of the acceptance notice. The end date is the end of the period stated in the landlord's offer notice as the period for the tenants to nominate a person to purchase on their behalf, or such later date as the landlord and tenants may agree (s. 6(4)(b)).

3.2 REQUISITE MAJORITY OF QUALIFYING TENANTS

The requisite majority of qualifying tenants means the requisite majority of the tenants in the building referred to in an offer notice under s. 5(1), or of the premises contained in a disposal referred to in s. 11(2), as appropriate.

The first step in identifying a requisite majority is to identify all the flats in the building or premises which are held by qualifying tenants. There is then one vote for each flat held by a qualifying tenant (s. 18A(3)). The total number of flats – and thus the total number of votes – is calculated as follows:

(a) in the case of a s. 5 offer notice, it is the total number of flats in the building let to qualifying tenants on the date when the period for accepting the offer expires;

(b) where the tenants are requesting information from a purchaser under s. 11A where there has been no s. 5 notice, it is the total number of flats let in the premises which are let to qualifying tenants at the date of their notice;

(c) if the notice is served under ss. 12A, 12B or 12C and there has been no s. 5 or s. 14 notice then the number is the total number of flats let in the premises let to qualifying tenants at the date of the notice.

3.3 THE NOMINATED PERSON

There is a definition of 'the nominated person' in s. 20(1) of the LTA 1987, but this adds very little. Section 6(5) provides that a person is 'duly nominated' for the purposes of this section if he is nominated at the same time as the acceptance notice is served, or before the expiry of the nomination period specified in the offer notice or any longer period agreed.

The Act is silent on the question of how this process of nomination should actually occur. The nominee can be any legal person or persons, whether corporate or unincorporate. The Act contains no clue as to how the tenants should arrive at the choice of a nominated person. In practice, the nominated person will usually be a company limited by shares purchased by the tenants for that precise purpose. In cases where there is a small number of purchasers then it may be as convenient for the property to be vested in them as trustees (s. 20(1) makes it clear that the nominated person may be more than one person).

A solicitor representing the tenants will sensibly hold a meeting with the tenants and also take written instructions from them. They will need to be advised on the constitution of the nominated person. Matters on which instructions will be needed include:

(a)   the sharing of the costs involved;
(b)   service shares and method of collection;
(c)   the directors and other officers of the nominated person.

3.4   FAILURE BY TENANTS TO ACCEPT OFFER OR MAKE NOMINATION

The landlord cannot dispose of the protected interest until the period for accepting the offer has expired without acceptance or the period for making a nomination has expired. Under s. 7 of the 1987 Act, if at the end of these periods no person has been nominated as the tenants' purchaser then the landlord may within 12 months dispose of the property as follows:

(a)   If the offer notice was a s. 5B notice (sale by public auction: see 2.6) then the sale must be by public auction and on the same terms as the offer notice (s. 7(2)).
(b)   For other disposals, the deposit and the consideration must be not less than those specified in the offer notice. This means *inter alia* that a reduced deposit cannot be accepted without a criminal offence being committed under s. 10A. The other terms must also correspond to those in the offer notice (s. 7(3)). This means that the material terms cannot be altered without a criminal offence being committed under s. 10A.

3.5   WHAT CAN BE DISPOSED OF?

The only interest which can be disposed of during the 12-month period specified in s. 7 is the protected interest which is the subject of the offer notice (s. 7(4)). Thus, s. 1(1) will apply to the disposal of any other interest unless it is not a relevant disposal (within s. 4). This, together with the remaining parts of s. 7, means that there is no scope for negotiation with a prospective purchaser of the terms of the disposal once an offer notice has been served. It is, of course, possible to serve a whole series of offer notices if this is practicable, although, of course, the landlord has to be willing to sell on the terms of each one or pay the costs of the tenants' abortive legal work (see s. 9B below at 3.6.2).

3.6 PROCEDURE AFTER A TENANTS' PURCHASER IS NOMINATED

Once the tenants have accepted the landlord's offer and nominated their purchaser then the landlord cannot sell to some other person except in accordance with the provisions dealing with a withdrawal by the nominated person (s. 9A: see 3.6.3.3) or a deemed withdrawal (s. 8A(5): see 3.6.3.2).

3.6.1 Landlord's withdrawal

Once the landlord has been served with the notice of nomination then it has a period of one month in which it can withdraw. This is done be service of a notice that it no longer wishes to proceed with the disposal (LTA 1987, s. 8(3)). There is no set form for this notice. A precedent is given in Appendix B. Once the landlord has served a notice under s. 8(3) it is not permitted to dispose of the property for a further 12 months from the date of service of the notice. In calculating this period 'month' will mean calendar month (Interpretation Act 1978, Sch. 5, and Law of Property Act 1925, s. 61). The 12-month period will then be calculated using the corresponding date rule. Because this rule is so useful it is set out in Appendix C.

3.6.2 Landlord's further obligations and right to withdraw

For disposals other than by auction, once the landlord is obliged to proceed it must comply with s. 8A of the LTA 1987. The procedures are as follows:

(a) The landlord must within a month of service of the nomination notice send a form of contract to the nominated person (LTA 1987, s. 8A(2)). No form is prescribed. The terms must conform with the offer notice. It is most straightforward to use a standard convey-ancing contract incorporating the standard conditions of sale and prepared in duplicate and in the usual way.

(b) If the landlord fails to provide a contract within the specified period it is deemed to have withdrawn and s. 9B applies (s. 8A(3)).

(c) The landlord may serve a notice of withdrawal under s. 9B at any time before a binding contract is entered into. If it does, it cannot dispose of the protected interest within 12 months of service of the offer notice. The landlord is responsible for the tenants' costs (s. 9B(4)) unless the withdrawal is before the end of the first four weeks of the nomination period specified in the offer notice (s. 9B(3)).

3.6.3 Nominated person's obligations

3.6.3.1 Nominated person's response
The nominated person has two months to respond after receipt of the contract. Within that period it must either withdraw or offer an exchange of contracts (LTA 1987, s. 8A(4)).

A withdrawal notice (see precedent, Appendix B) need not follow any prescribed form. If the nominated person does not withdraw it must '. . . offer an exchange of contracts, that is to say, sign the contract and send it to the landlord, together with the requisite deposit' (s. 8A(4)(b)). For this purpose the requisite deposit is that stated in the contract or (if it is less) 10 per cent of the consideration

The question may arise as to when the 'offer' to exchange contracts is actually made. It can scarcely be said that the nominated person offers an exchange of contracts unless that offer is known to the landlord. In principle, then, it seems that this will be done on the day the signed contact and deposit are delivered to the landlord. There cannot within s. 8A(4)(b) be an effective offer of exchange unless the signed contract is sent together with the deposit.

3.6.3.2 Failure to act or withdrawal by nominated person
Section 8A(5) operates if the nominated person either serves a notice of withdrawal or fails to offer an exchange of contracts complying with s. 8A(4) within the relevant period. The effect is that there is then a deemed withdrawal by the nominated person.

3.6.3.3 Nominated person's notice of withdrawal
The nominated person is given by s. 9A(1) a right to withdraw at any time. If the nominated person becomes aware that the number of qualifying tenants 'desiring to proceed' is less than the requisite majority' then it must forthwith serve a withdrawal notice. There is no form of notice specified. A suggested form is found at Form 15 in Appendix B.

Once a withdrawal notice has been served then the landlord can proceed to dispose of the protected interest to someone other than the nominated person. This right lasts for 12 months from the service of the withdrawal notice. The disposal must satisfy the conditions laid down in s. 9A(4) and (5).

Where the offer notice was one to which s. 5B applies (sale by auction: see 2.6), the disposal must be by a public auction sale on the terms specified in the offer notice (s. 9A(4)). In any other case the deposit and consideration must be at least the figures specified in the offer notice or any higher figure agreed by the landlord and the nominated person. Such agreement includes an agreement subject to contract (s. 9A(5)(a)).

3.6.3.4 *Costs consequence of withdrawal notice*

The burden of costs depends on the stage at which the withdrawal notice is served. If it is before the end of the first four weeks of the nomination period specified in the offer notice then the tenants are not liable for any of the landlord's costs (s. 9A(6)). If the withdrawal notice is served after this period then the landlord may recover any costs reasonably incurred in connection with the disposal between the end of that four-week period and service of the withdrawal notice. Such costs can be recovered from the nominated person and the qualifying tenants (s. 9A(7)). This subsection adds, 'Any such liability of the nominated person and those tenants is a joint and several liability.' This clearly allows the landlord to proceed to recover the costs from such of the tenants and the nominated person as it chooses. The costs will be recoverable by a default action in the county court.

3.6.4 Exchange of contracts

If the landlord fails to complete the exchange of contracts within seven days of receipt of the contract from the nominated person then there is a deemed withdrawal by the landlord (LTA 1987, s. 8A(6)). If the nominated person sends the contract by post or document exchange then, if the contract is subject to the Standard Conditions of Sale (SCS), SCS 2.1.2 will apply and 'the contract is made when the last copy is posted or deposited at the document exchange' as the case may be. If the Standard Conditions have not been used and the contract is silent on this point then if the offer is by post the exchange will still be complete when the seller's part is posted (*Adams* v *Lindsell* (1881) 1 B and Ald 681).

3.7 ASSIGNMENT COVENANTS

There will be many cases where the disposal which the landlord wishes to make is constrained by a requirement for consent to be obtained, or even by an absolute prohibition on assignment.

3.7.1 Absolute covenants

The landlord may be disposing of an interest which is subject to an absolute prohibition against assignment. Where there is such a condition an assignment in breach of the condition may still pass the relevant legal interest (see *Governors of the Peabody Donation Fund* v *Higgins* [1993] 3 All ER 122. There is no particular provision of the Act relevant to these unusual circumstances.

3.7.2 Qualified covenants

The landlord may be disposing of an interest which is subject to a qualified covenant against assignment. In this case s. 8E(1) of the 1987 Act is applicable. It requires the landlord to use its best endeavours to obtain consent for the disposal and, if it appears that the person is 'obliged not to withhold his consent unreasonably but has nevertheless so withheld it', to start proceedings for a declaration. Section 8E(1) does not apply (s. 8E(2)) if the landlord serves a notice of withdrawal under s. 9A or s. 9B, or the landlord's offer lapses under s. 10 (see 3.9). In practice a landlord faced with the possibility of legal action under s. 8E(1) will be most likely to serve a notice of withdrawal.

However, cases may occur where a landlord complies with its duty under s. 8E(1) and no consent is still forthcoming (say because it is refused on reasonable grounds such as the financial inadequacy of the nominated person). In this case s. 8E(3) will apply. The landlord must serve a notice on the nominated person telling it what has happened (see Form 14, Appendix B). Once this notice has been served the landlord may in the 12 months from the date of service of the notice dispose of the protected interest in accordance with s. 8E(4) and s. 8E(5). These subsections allow the landlord to dispose of the interest by auction under s. 8E(4) if the original offer notice was one in respect of an auction under s. 5B and provided that the other terms correspond to those in the offer notice; and in any other case under s. 8E(5) if the deposit and consideration are not less than those specified in the office notice or as agreed between the landlord and the nominated person, and provided that the other terms are as set out in the offer notice.

3.8 ONCE THERE IS A BINDING CONTRACT

There can be no withdrawal under s. 9A once there is a binding contract between the landlord and the nominated person (LTA 1987, s. 9A(8)). This contract should then be completed in the same way as any other conveyancing contract. The solicitor asking for the tenants will take the same steps by way of searches and investigations of title as is usual in conveyancing. The contract is registerable as a C(iv) land change, or by notice or caution in the Land Registry. Because this contract arises in contentious circumstances registration might be especially advisable.

3.9 LAPSE OF LANDLORD'S OFFER

Section 10 of the 1987 Act operates if after the landlord has served an offer notice the premises cease to be qualifying premises (this may happen if the number of flats held by qualifying tenants falls below the required number: (see 3.2).

Once s. 10(1) applies the landlord may serve a notice (a 'cessation notice') on the qualifying tenants. This will state that the premises have ceased to be qualifying premises and accordingly that the offer notice and any subsequent steps are to be treated as not having occurred (for a form of notice, see Form 17, Appendix B).

A cessation notice is effectively served it is served:

(a)   on all the qualifying tenants;
(b)   on at least 90 per cent of the qualifying tenants; or
(c)   if there are fewer than ten, on all but one of the qualifying tenants.

Under s. 10(3), if the landlord does not serve a cessation notice then the Act continues to apply as though the premises were still within the Act. This poses an apparent problem if there are no qualifying tenants on whom the landlord can serve a cessation notice. However, if this should happen then the nominated person is obliged to serve a withdrawal notice under s. 9A(2). This does not mean, of course, that the nominated person necessarily will serve a withdrawal notice, and doubtless curious situations may arise if it does not. It may be noted that the criminal offence of failing to comply with the requirement of this legislation can be committed by a landlord, but not by a tenant.

CHAPTER FOUR

Enforcement Against Purchasers

4.1 INTRODUCTION

It was common after Part I of the 1987 Act was in force for perfectly respectable property companies to choose not to comply with it. Deliberate non-compliance will now be unlikely because it leads to the commission of a criminal offence (by virtue of s. 10A inserted by the Housing Act 1996, s. 91). This is dealt with in the following chapter. Nevertheless, there will be cases when by oversight (or perhaps deliberately) a landlord has not complied with the Act. Should this happen then the tenants have certain statutory rights against the purchaser. The disposal itself is not affected (see LTA 1987, s. 10A(5)).

4.2 RIGHT TO INFORMATION

The tenants should receive notice from any purchaser that the purchase has been effected. The purchaser will do this otherwise it is not entitled to receive rent from the tenants. The landlord will also be guilty of a summary offence (see Landlord and Tenant Act 1985, ss. 3 and 3A; 1987 Act, ss. 47–49). Once the tenants are aware of a purchase they may request details of it by serving a notice under s. 11A of the 1987 Act. A form of notice is found at Form 18, Appendix B.

The notice must be served on behalf of the majority of qualifying tenants and must give the name and address of a person to whom the information must be given (s. 11A(2)). This can be, for example, the solicitor acting on behalf of the nominated tenants. There are no other formal requirements for this notice.

Section 11A(3) imposes a time within which the notice must be served. The court has no power to relieve from a failure to serve a notice in time. The notice must be served within four months of either of two events specified in s. 11A(3):

(a) If s. 3A of the Landlord and Tenant Act 1985 applies, the event is service of the statutory notices on the requisite majority of qualifying tenants. This provision applies wherever the interest of the Landlord 'is assigned'. Section 3A is set out in Appendix D. It should be noted that so far as registered land is concerned an assignment takes place only upon registration (*Brown & Root Technology Ltd* v *Sun Alliance and London Assurance Co. Ltd* [1997] 18 EG 123, CA). This decision concerns the meaning of 'assignment' in the breach clause in a lease. But the reasoning of the court was that there was 'no transfer (and therefore no assignment) of the legal title to the lease' until registration. The logic of this decision is that there is no requirement to serve a statutory notice until a transfer (whether of a landlord's freehold or leasehold) is perfected by registration.

(b) If s. 3A of the 1985 Act does not apply then the relevant event is the receipt by the tenant of documents which satisfy s. 11A(3)(b) of the 1987 Act. This requires the documents both to inform the tenants that the original disposal has taken place and to alert them to the existence of their rights of pre-emption and the timescale for the exercise of these rights.

4.3   COMPLIANCE BY PURCHASER

A person served with a notice under s. 11A of the LTA 1987 must comply within one month of its service (s. 11A(4)). The obligation is to give particulars of the terms of the disposal (s. 11A(1)(a)). The particulars must include any deposit or consideration required for the disposal. The term 'required' is used deliberately in order to oblige the purchaser to provide these details of the sums which are terms of the disposal whether or not they have been paid in fact. If the disposal was on contract then a copy of the contract must be provided (s. 11A(1)(b)). The Court of Appeal in *Staszewki* v *Maribella Ltd* [1998] 04 EG 149 discussed what the requirements were for compliance with s. 11 (this was a case on the Act before it was amended by the Housing Act 1996). If there is a contract and a disposal on different terms then this must be made clear. The information could be contained in more than one document given on more than one date. The notice need not state that it is a s. 11 notice but it must be clear that it is. In *Staszewki v Maribella* the landlord's solicitor's prevaricated when asked if the information supplied complied with s. 11. The court held that ... 'It is incumbent upon a landlord to make clear the purpose for which the notice has been served'. Saying clearly in the notice that it is served in compliance with s. 11 obviously best does this (see also *Belvedere Court Ltd* v *Frogmore Ltd* [1996] 1 All ER 312, referring to a s. 16 notice).

4.4 RIGHT TO TAKE BENEFIT OF CERTAIN TRANSACTIONS

The circumstances in which the tenants can take over the benefit of disposals by the landlord are dealt with in the LTA 1987, ss. 12A, 12B and 12C. They have certain common provisions which will be discussed first.

4.4.1 Notice by qualifying tenants

In each case the qualifying tenants must claim their statutory rights by a notice served on the landlord by the requisite majority of qualifying tenants (see 3.2). The notice must specify who is the nominated person to act on behalf of the tenants (s. 12D(1)). Because the nominated person cannot readily be changed, some thought should be given by the tenants' advisers as to who this should be. In most cases the tenants will establish a management company for this purpose.

4.4.2 Role of nominated person

Because the nominated person must be specified in a notice under ss. 12A, 12B or 12C, the tenants will need to come to an agreement as to who will be the nominated person before serving notice under any of these sections upon the landlord.

A rather odd provision in s. 12D(2) says that the nominated person can be replaced 'if, and only if, he has (for any reason) ceased to be able to act as a nominated person'. The 1987 Act contains no explanation of what ceasing to be able to act involves. Does it mean a lack of legal capacity, such as a company which is struck off the register or a natural person who loses mental capacity? Clearly these cases must come within the subsection. More dubious are situations where through tiredness, inefficiency, age, infirmity of the body or otherwise the nominated person (or the tenants on his behalf) believes that it is effectively a case of inability to act. It would take strong argument to convince a court that such circumstances amounted to inability in law.

The purpose of s. 12D(2) is to prevent the tenants using their statutory rights to speculate in the property by exercising the option and then negotiating a subsale to finance it.

4.4.3 More than one nominated person

In most cases the nominated person will be a company set up or purchased by the tenants for that purpose. There may be cases where, instead, two or more of their number are chosen to hold the purchased estate as trustees. In this case they will hold the estate which they purchase on a trust of land under the Trusts of Land and Appointment of Trustees Act 1996. Section 12D(3) of the LTA 1987 provides that in such a case where any of the trustees cease to act without being replaced the remainder may continue to act as the nominated person. Like so much of this Act, this provision is oddly drafted. It seems to suggest that the usual statutory provisions for the appointment of new trustees do not apply to the nominated person.

4.4.4 Costs against the nominated person

A costs order may be made against the nominated person either by the court or by the Lands Tribunal. The detailed provisions are dealt with in chapter 6. Any such award of costs imposed by virtue of s. 12D(4) of the 1987 Act is a joint and several liability upon the nominated person and the qualifying tenant(s) by whom the relevant notice is served. This is an important point as it puts each qualifying tenant potentially at risk for the whole of the costs. This point must be made when advising tenants.

4.5 TIME FOR EXERCISE OF RIGHT

Sections 12A, 12B and 12C have very similar timescales within which the tenants must serve a notice exercising their right. The period is within six months of the date of the purchaser's compliance with a s. 11A notice or, if no s. 11A notice is served, within six months of the majority of the qualifying tenants being served with documents informing them of the original disposal, their rights under the Act and the timescale for exercising them (see s. 12A(2); s. 12B(3); s. 12C(3)). If the disposal is one to which s. 12B applies then the timescale is varied where the tenants do not serve a s. 11A notice by giving the tenants (in cases where s. 3A of the Landlord and Tenant Act 1985 applies: see 4.2) six months from the service of the s. 3A notice.

4.6   SECTION 12A NOTICES: TAKING THE BENEFIT OF A CONTRACT

4.6.1   Right of qualifying tenants to take benefit of contract

By serving a notice under s. 12A of the LTA 1987, the tenants can elect that a contract entered into by the landlord will have effect as if it is made with their nominated person.

The nominated person is required to meet any requirements as to the deposit (s. 12A(3)(a)) and fulfil any other condition required to be fulfilled by the purchaser on entering the contract. (s. 12A(3)(b)). The notice given under s. 12A is of no effect unless these two conditions are fulfilled.

Time limits in the contract (subject to agreement to the contrary) start to run again on service of the tenants' notice (s. 12A(4)). However, the same subsection provides that nothing in the contract as given effect to by s. 12A requires the completion date to be before the end of 28 days after the nominated person is desired to have entered the contract.   .

4.6.2   Contract includes property outside the Act or more than one building within the Act

Section 12A(5) deals with the situation where the original disposal includes property in addition to premises to which the Act applies. The tenants in this case have a choice. They may specify in their notice the property which they wish to acquire and the relevant terms on which they wish to acquire it, or they may in the notice require the property and the terms to be determined by a leasehold valuation tribunal.

The legislation does not deal expressly with the situation where the contract includes more than one building within the Act. Where the buildings are on one estate the tenants of them collectively may choose to purchase all the buildings concerned. It is very likely that the court will allow them to do so. If the contract includes buildings on different sites then to make sense of the Act the tenants of each building must be able to serve a s. 12A notice in respect of their building.

Any dispute as to the validity of a s. 12A(5) notice must be decided by the court, but the leasehold valuation tribunal must decide any dispute about the effect of a notice served under s. 12A(5). The jurisdiction of the leasehold valuation tribunal is confined to the specific issues mentioned, i.e. determining the property and terms of the transaction where the s. 12A notice requests it to do so, and determining any issue as to the matter specified is a notice under s. 13 (see chapter 6).

In *Denetower Ltd* v *Toop* [1991] 3 All ER 661, the Court upheld the validity of a purchase notice, which included property the tenants had no right to acquire. The Court of Appeal held that the words claiming the property described it subject to 'such modifications as are necessary'. The notice gave adequate indication of the claim. A draftsman could not be expected to describe the property exactly.

In *Kay Green* v *Twinsectra Ltd* [1996] 4 All ER 546, the Court of Appeal had to consider the validity of a purchase notice. The Court decided that the essential ingredients of a purchase notice are that it 'must be in writing and served upon the new landlord in time. Further, it must give adequate notice of the requirement of the qualifying tenants to have the estate or interest in the premises, as defined in s. 1, transferred to a nominated person' (Aldous LJ at p. 569). Other requirements of s. 12 (as it was then) were directory only.

The notice was not invalidated, simply by the fact that it contained extra property. The Court held clearly upheld the right of the tenants to purchase more than one building by a purchase notice: '... the notice served was a valid notice by the qualifying tenants of buildings 1 and 4 of Tudor Court and of Tudor House. In these circumstances, I would allow this appeal in so far as it relates to the tenants of those buildings' (p. 561).

Regrettably, both the Act and the case law give a very unclear picture of how tenants should be advised to proceed where the landlord has disposed of a 'job lot' of buildings. If the tenants of several buildings disposed of together wish to purchase them all together then a purchase notice served on behalf of them all would seem to be valid. However, it is perfectly in order to use the same nominated purchaser for several buildings in separate purchase notices, and that is probably the safest course. If it is not apparent what is the exact extent of the property to be purchased then the purchase notice can properly contain a saving clause such as that in *Kay Green* v *Twinsectra Ltd* [1997] 23 EG 146 (a leasehold valuation case involving the same parties as the case last cited) – 'such of the premises as falls within s. 1 of the Landlord and Tenant Act 1987'. Where a landlord has been in default, both the courts and the leasehold valuation tribunal have accepted a purchase notice which deals with more than one building – a recent example is *Ground Premium Property Management Ltd* v *Longmint Ltd* [1998] 11 EG 183.

4.6.3 Rights over other land

The tenants may be able to acquire any other appurtenant land over which they have rights (see *Denetower Ltd* v *Toop* [1991] 3 All ER 661). Alternatively they may be given perpetual rights over features such as gardens and amenity land (see *Twinsectra Ltd* v *Jones* [1998] 23 EG 134). In that case the Lands Tribunal thought it proper to grant such perpetual rights even though the tenants held them subject to the landlord's power to determine them. The crucial factor was that the landlord purported to terminate these rights after the purchase notice had been served. This case was on the 1987 Act before it was amended by the Housing Act 1996. The relevant provision was s. 12, now replaced by s. 12A to s. 12D. Though the wording is slightly different, *Twinsectra* v *Jones* should remain good law.

Problems will inevitably arise, however, where the landlord attempts to exclude from the sale areas which the tenants enjoy, such as gardens, sports facilities and so on. A typical factual situation is found in *Kay Green* v *Twinsectra Ltd* [1997] 23 EG 146. The tenants in the relevant flats occupied on terms which gave them rights to enjoy the garden and amenity land subject to notice of termination by the landlord. The decision is only that of a leasehold valuation tribunal, so it is of significance primarily as an illustration of how the Act operates. The tribunal in *Twinsectra* decided that the Act did

allow us to include within the transfer the rights given to the tenants in their leases but not subject to termination by Twinsectra. We are satisfied from the reasoning in *Denetower* that easements are rights which can be compulsorily acquired as appurtenances under Part I, by analogy with Part III. If the original vendors had complied with their statutory duty [as was found to be so in this case in the Court of Appeal] to offer the freeholds to the tenants, the tenants would have received with the freehold the appurtenant right to use the gardens and amenity land in accordance with their leases. Had they done so, the owner of the freehold of the land would in our view have met with insuperable difficulties had it tried to restrict their rights, the right to determine them having passed to the applicant with the freehold.

This case was, however, concerned with the leasehold valuation tribunal's powers under s. 13 of the Act. Section 13 has in fact been drastically amended by the Housing Act 1996 and, accordingly, this point has to be looked at again in the light of the amendments. It is clear from other cases that the Court regarded the role of the leasehold valuation tribunal in determining what property was to be included in a purchase as crucial. These cases are *Kay Green* v *Twinsectra Ltd* [1996] 4 All ER 546 and *Belvedere Court Management Ltd* v *Frogmore Developments Ltd* [1996] 1 All ER 312. They both concern cases under the 1987 Act before the sweeping amendments made under the 1996 Act. It is implicit in them both that purchases can include outbuildings, amenity land and gardens, though it is not made clear how this result is reached. The difficulty is made more vivid by taking an example. In *Twinsectra*, the rights in question were determinable by the landlord. Once the tenants acquired the freehold the view of the tribunal was clearly that in reality they (as owners of the freehold) would have the benefit of the right to determine the lease-holders' ancillary rights. However, suppose the facts were these: Attlee Buildings is occupied by 20 leasehold tenants who have the right to walk through Butler Building to use the swimming pool in Canning Building. If the freeholder wishes to sell the freehold of Attlee Buildings to Disraeli Ltd, it must first offer it to the tenants. That offer will be, we assume, solely for the freehold of Attlee Buildings. The tenants have no right to accept any offer except the one that is made. In consequence, if they accept this offer then they will purchase the freehold of Attlee Building and retain whatever leasehold easements and rights they have over Butler and Canning. Neither the court nor the leasehold valuation tribunal will in these circumstances have any jurisdiction to turn the offer by Attlee into one which includes freehold easements over Butler and Canning. Buried in this analysis is the possibility of devising a scheme for avoiding the Act, and this is returned to below (chapter 5).

4.7   SECTION 12B NOTICES: RIGHT TO COMPEL SALE ETC. BY PURCHASER

4.7.1   The 'purchase notice'

A s. 12B notice (a 'purchase notice') will be used where the property has been conveyed to a purchaser, whether pursuant to a contract or otherwise. The notice requires the purchaser to convey the property subject to the disposal to the nominated person 'on the terms on which it was made (including those relating to the consideration payable)' (s. 12B(2)).

The main area of difficulty with such a notice will be where s. 12B(4) applies, i.e. where the notice related to 'other property in addition to premises to which this Part' of the Act applied. There are two areas of difficulty:

(a)   Where the other property is outside Part I of the 1987 Act, the tenants may in their s. 12B notice either specify the subject matter which they claim and the terms on which the disposal is to be made, or insist that these matters be referred to the leasehold valuation tribunal.

(b)   If the sale has been of more than one building within the Act then the Act is unhelpful. The commentary on the same situation when dealing with s. 12A notice should be referred to (see 4.6.2 above).

4.7.2 Discharge of incumbrances

It may happen that since the original disposal the property has become subject to an incumbrance. In this case s. 12B(5) operates. There are two separate provisions. The first deals with charges on the property. Section 12B(5)(a) applies to charges on the property whether the charge is to secure the payment of money or the performance of another obligation. It applies to mortgages and liens but does not apply to a rentcharge (s. 12B(6)). The effect of s. 12B(5)(a) is that the transfer to the nominated person will discharge the property from the charge. Schedule 1 of the 1987 Act contains detailed provisions dealing with the discharge of mortgages. The nominated person has to apply the purchase money towards such charges in order of their priority. It appears that this obligation does not apply to floating charges (Sch. 1, para. 2(3)) and the property will simply be discharged from any floating charge. If there is a debenture which is a specific charge then (depending on its priority) the purchase money must be applied towards its discharge so far as it goes (Sch. 1, para. 2 (4)).

In determining the amount of a charge, no right to consolidate the charge with another charge is permitted (Sch. 1, para. 3). So far as the actual amount payable on redemption is concerned, Sch. 1, para. 3(2) must be considered. It provides for the amount of notice in lieu of interest to be paid and overrides the terms of the charge where they are different from the effect of the schedule. The provisions may, however, entitle a mortgagee to compensation if it has to re-invest on worse terms.

If there are difficulties in ascertaining the amount to be repaid then the nominated person may make a payment into court (Sch. 1, para. 4).

Incumbrances other than charges are dealt with separately by s. 12B(5)(b). Where incumbrances other then charges have been created then the property is disposed of subject to the incumbrance but at a lower consideration to reflect the amount by which the incumbrance reduces the value of the property. The meaning of 'incumbrance' was considered by the Court of Appeal in *Belvedere Court Management Ltd* v *Frogmore Developments Ltd* [1996] 1 All ER 312. A lease of a flat granted after the disposal would be an incumbrance. An overriding or reversionary lease is not an incumbrance. This case highlights the fact that the Act gives tenants the right of pre-emption when there is a disposal of the reversionary lease. This is explained by Lord Bingham MR (at p. 327):

> . . . where a new immediate landlord grants a lease which has the effect of transferring the reversion of tenants' leases from himself to another immediate landlord, the former must be regarded as no longer holding the estate or interest that has been the subject matter of the original disposal.

The effect is that any disposition of the immediate reversion, whether by the grant of a lease or freeholder transfer, is a disposal with the Act.

4.7.3 Change in value of property

Section 12B(7) deals with the situation where the value of the property increases after the original disposal. In this case the consideration payable is 'the amount that might reasonable have been obtained on a corresponding disposal made on the open market at the time of the original disposal if the change in circumstances had already taken place' (s. 12B(7), replaced s. 12(6) of the 1987 Act by virtue of the amendments made in the Housing Act 1996). The wording in the old s. 12(6) was discussed in detail in *Twinsectra Ltd v Jones* [1998] 23 EG 134 by the Lands Tribunal in a fully reasoned judgment. Section 12(6) referred to a change in value 'at any time since the original disposal'. Section 12(B)(7) refers to an increase in value 'since the original disposal'. The words 'at any time' are thus missing. They seem, however, to be mere surplusage and *Twinsectra* is probably good law. It decides that increases in the value of property, as such, which occur after the service of the purchase notice, are ignored. Thus, where a relegated tenant died after service of the purchase notice the price payable was increased by the fact that the flat had vacant possession. The Tribunal decided that changes up to the date of the contract or conveyance must be taken into account. The valuation date is the time of the original disposal and there is no provision for interest. This possibility of the consideration changing (in a large block of flats quite often) makes negotiation difficult. The Lands Tribunal said of this:

> If numerous changes of circumstances occur after the tenant's purchase notice, then the procedures leading to the eventual disposal could be lengthy and cumbersome. In practice, however, I suspect that this objection to the interpretation which I have adopted may be more apparent then real. (p. 143)

4.7.4 Content of notice

A suitable notice is reproduced at Appendix B, Form 20. The notice need not specify the subject matter of the disposal or the terms but may provide for those matters to be determined by a leasehold valuation tribunal.

4.8 SECTION 12C NOTICES: SURRENDER BY LANDLORD

A s. 12C notice is used when the original disposal is a surrender by the landlord of a tenancy held by it.

An express surrender is required to be by deed (Law of Property Act 1925, s. 52). A surrender by operation of law (excepted from s. 52 by s. 52(2)(c)) is a much looser concept. Case law on whether particular acts of the parties evidence a surrender is not uncommon. It will be apparent to the tenants that their landlord's lease has terminated because rent will become payable to the superior title holder. However, it will not be apparent whether this is the result of a surrender (to which s. 12C of the 1987 Act applies), or of a forfeiture or disclaimer (to which it does not). This can be discovered by serving a notice under s. 11A (see 4.2).

4.8.1 Effect of notice

The effect of the notice is to entitle the requisite majority to have a new lease granted to the person they nominate. The terms are 'the same' as the tenancy which has been surrendered, and the length of the term is such that it will expire on the same date as that tenancy would have expired. Any consideration paid for the original surrender must be paid by the nominated person (LTA 1987, s. 12C(4)).

4.8.2 Where tenancy surrendered included other property

If the tenancy surrender included premises to which the LTA 1987, Part I did not apply then the s. 12C notice must request only a tenancy of the premises to which the Act applies (s. 12C(5)). The notes on s. 12A notices at 4.6 above may be of help in such a case.

4.9 DISPUTES BEFORE LEASEHOLD VALUATION TRIBUNALS

The jurisdiction of the leasehold valuation tribunals to deal with issues under Part I of the LTA 1987 is contained in s. 13. There are two areas in which the tribunals are involved:

(a) disputes about matters specified in a notice under ss. 12A, 12B or 12C (s. 13(1)(a)). This gives the tribunals a specific but clearly limited jurisdiction. The extent of this (under the section before it was amended by the Housing Act 1996) was discussed in *134 Shirland Road Management Co. Ltd* v *Lester* [1997] 97 EG 49;

(b) any matters mentioned in ss. 8C(4), 12A(5) or 12B(4). These again are very specific issues:

(i) s. 8C(4) – this is the determination of the monetary value of a non-monetary consideration,

    (ii)   s. 12A(5) – where tenants claim to take the benefit of a contract which contains property to which Part I of the Act does not apply the leasehold valuation tribunal has power to determine the terms of the contract applicable to the tenants (see 4.6.2),

    (iii) s. 12B(4) – where tenants claim to take the benefit of a disposition under s. 12B and that disposition relates to property to which Part I of the Act does not apply then the leasehold valuation tribunal has power to determine the terms of the disposition to the tenants (see 4.7.1).

The procedures for litigation under the Act are further discussed in chapter 6.

4.10 RIGHTS OF QUALIFYING TENANTS AGAINST SUBSEQUENT PURCHASER

There may be cases where the landlord has disposed of an interest within Part I of the 1987 Act but by the time the tenants are able to act the purchaser no longer holds the relevant interest. In this case s. 16 of the Act may enable the tenants to enforce their rights against a subsequent purchaser. For s. 16 to apply:

    (a) a notice must be served under one of ss. 11A, 12A, 12B or 12C. The tenants may in fact know all they need to know in order to have to rely upon s. 16. Yet a relevant notice must be served on the original purchaser;

    (b) at the time that notice is served the purchaser must no longer hold 'the estate or interest that was the subject-matter of the original disposal' (s. 16(1)).

4.10.1 Steps to be taken by original purchaser

Where s. 16 applies the original purchaser has to act as follows if it is served with a notice under the Act:

    (a) Where a s. 11A notice is served there are two steps which the purchaser must take:

        (i)   s. 16(2)(a) requires notice to be given to the person named in the s. 11A notice of the name and address of the new purchaser ('the subsequent purchaser'),

(ii)   s. 16(2)(b) requires a copy of the s. 11A notice and the reply given under s. 16(1) to be served on the subsequent purchaser.

(b)   Where a notice under ss. 12A, 12B or 12C is served then s. 16(3) requires the original purchaser to forward the notice to the subsequent purchaser and to serve the nominated person with the name and address of the subsequent purchaser.

4.10.2   Purchaser disposes of part

The original purchaser may in some cases dispose of part only of the property or interest purchased. In this case s. 16(5) applies. The effect is that the tenants can use ss. 12A to 14 against the original purchaser and the subsequent purchaser in respect of the part they each own.

It is not necessary in order for this provision to operate that the part in question should in itself meet the qualifying conditions to be premises under this Act. Thus, an original purchaser may buy a block of flats and its grounds and quickly sell the grounds on to a subsequent purchaser. The tenants may use s. 16 – in particular s. 16(5) – to recover the grounds from the subsequent purchaser.

4.11   TERMINATION OF RIGHTS AGAINST PURCHASER

4.11.1   Premises no longer premises to which Part I applies

Section 17 is of use to a purchaser or subsequent purchaser when a notice has been served under any of ss. 11A, 12A, 12B or 12C. It enables the purchaser (or any subsequent purchaser) to serve a notice on the qualifying tenants informing then that the premises in question are no longer premises to which Part I of the 1987 Act applies. Such a notice is reproduced at Form 23, Appendix B.

A notice is effectively served either if it is served on 90 per cent of the tenants or (if there are fewer then ten) on all but one of them.

4.11.2   Inaction by tenants

Tenants may begin the process of exercising the rights under the 1987 Act against a purchaser and then the matter may fail to proceed due to the tenants' inaction or the landlord's intransigence. In the latter case the tenants must instigate action in the court or before the leasehold valuation tribunal. If the delay is caused by the tenants' inaction then the purchaser can serve a notice under s. 17(3) or (4), the effect of which is that the tenants lose their rights to proceed against the purchaser. It is thus very important for the tenants' advisers to observe the timescales laid down by s. 17. If there is no contract with the purchaser within three months of service of the s. 12A, s. 12B or s. 12C notice then an application must be made to the court or leasehold valuation tribunal. If such an application has been made then, unless a contract is entered into with two months of its determination, another application must be made. If these steps are not taken then the tenants risk losing their opportunity to proceed against the purchaser.

4.12 PROSPECTIVE PURCHASER NOTICE

The marginal note to s. 18 is 'Notices served by prospective purchasers to ensure that rights of first refusal do not arise'. The purpose of the section is to allow a prospective purchaser to serve notices on the tenants to inform them of the prospective purchase. If they do not reply or if they indicate their lack of interest then the disposal is treated as one to which Part I of the 1987 Act does not apply.

There is clearly some possibility that a landlord might reasonably think that a disposal is not within the Act, but a prospective purchaser could have a contrary view or be in doubt in this matter. In such a case a purchaser may find the s. 18 procedure a useful way of avoiding any potential problems with the tenants.

The procedure in using a s. 18 notice is as follows:

(a) A s. 18 notice is reproduced as Form 27 in Appendix B.
(b) The notice to be served by a prospective purchaser is different from an offer notice under s. 5 (see chapter 2).
(c) In order to gain the benefit of s. 18, the notices must be served on at least 80 per cent of the tenants of the flats affected (s. 18(3)).
(d) The expression 'tenants' under s. 18 does not mean qualifying tenants. This is made abundantly clear by s. 18(4). However, s. 18(4) introduces an element of the surreal into the definition of 'a tenant'. It states:

> (4) For the purposes of subsection (3) each of the flats affected shall be regarded as having one tenant, who shall count towards any of the percentages specified in that subsection whether he is a qualifying tenant of the flat or not.

If this curious provision is taken literally then each flat in the affected building is assumed to have one tenant whether it has any tenants or not. It may be vacant, it may be occupied by or on behalf of the landlord. The more likely purpose of s. 18 is that it is meant to mean, 'every tenanted flat in the building is assumed to have one tenant'. This prevents the overweighting in any alleged majority of flats which are owned by joint tenants. However this is not what s. 18(4) actually says, and the effect of the odd literal meaning will be returned to below.

(e) The tenants have two months to reply to the notice (s. 18(3)(a) – note that the period of 28 days in the Act was amended to two months by the Tenants' Rights of First Refusal (Amendment) Regulations 1996, SI 1996 No. 2371).

Section 18 bites if the conditions of s. 18(3) are satisfied. First 80 per cent of the tenants of flats affected must have been served. Service can have a sensible meaning only if the flats actually have a tenant. On the literal wording of s. 18(4) every flat is deemed to have one tenant – this means even empty flats must be served! Secondly, neither s. 18(3)(a) nor s. 18(3)(b) must be satisfied:

(a) s. 18(3)(a) – the condition is that not more than 50 per cent of the tenants served have served a notice in reply under s. 18(2)(b).

(b) s. 18(3)(b) – the condition is extremely badly worded. What seems to be required is that more than 50 per cent of the tenants served have replied and the replies of at least 50 per cent of those served state that the tenant does not regard himself as entitled to a s. 5 notice or would not wish to exercise the right of first refusal if none was served. Section 18(3)(b) is regrettably poorly constructed. A literal meaning could be that where more than 50 per cent of the tenants served with a s. 18 notice have replied, all the reply notices must be ones not from tenants who are claiming the right to receive s. 5 notices or avail themselves of them if served. This construction arises from the rather odd wording – 'the notices in each case indicate that the tenant serving it either ... does not [claim the benefit of s. 5] or ... would not ... avail himself [of it]'. The words in each case in italics do seem to suggest clearly that every notice must be a negative one. But that construction is nonsensical. If less than 50 per cent reply then s. 18(3)(a) is satisfied even if a large number of replies are positive. Thus, to have any sense in the provisions, s. 18(3)(b) must contemplate a situation where some replies may be positive. The proper reading must refer to 50 per cent of those actually served (being over 80 per cent of the tenants) giving non-positive replies.

4.13   ENFORCEMENT OF THE ACT

Section 19 of the LTA 1987 gives the court power to order compliance with the duties imposed by the Act. Any person 'interested' may apply for an order. This could be a qualifying tenant, a representative body of qualifying tenants and possibly some other person with an interest in the relevant building or premises.

4.14   TENANTS' RIGHTS AS PROPERTY RIGHTS

It seems to have been accepted by the Court of Appeal in *Crumpton et al* v *Unifox Properties Ltd et al* (1992) 25 HLR 121, that the tenant's right of pre-emption is an overriding interest within s. 70(1)(g) of the Land Registration Act 1925. The relevance of this is somewhat elusive. A purchaser and a subsequent purchaser are intended to be subject to the tenant's rights by virtue of the complex provisions of Part I of the 1987 Act. In principle it would seem that the right to operate these statutory procedures should be cloaked in the status of 'property rights' within s. 70(1)(g) of the 1925 Act. The *locus classicus* is *National Provincial Bank* v *Ainsworth* [1965] AC 1125. The hallmark of such rights is in Runcie LJ's statement (made in the Court of Appeal but approved in the House of Lords that:

> It seems to me that section 70 in all its parts is dealing with rights in reference to land which have the quality of being capable of enduring through different ownership's of the land, according to normal conceptions of title to real property.

The tenant's rights clearly fall within this rubric.

CHAPTER FIVE

Avoidance and Criminal Offences

5.1 CRIMINAL OFFENCES

5.1.1 Failure to comply with requirements of Part I

A landlord can commit a criminal offence under s. 10A of the LTA 1987. In order to do so it must make a relevant disposal. The offence is committed if it makes such a disposal either:

- (a) without complying with the requirements of s. 5 as to the service of notices; or
- (b) in breach of any prohibition or restriction imposed by ss. 6 to 10.

It should be noted that this provision is widely drafted. It may be infringed by a quite minor example of non-compliance with ss. 5 to 10. For example, making a relevant disposal on contractual terms that are slightly different from the terms in the offer notice, or failing to serve some of the qualifying tenants.

5.1.2 The defence of reasonable excuse

There is a general defence to the offence in s. 10A, in that the infringement is committed only if the breach is made 'without reasonable excuse'.

Once the defence is raised by the facts or put in evidence by the defendant then the onus is on the prosecution to disprove it. Thus, it may be said the evidential burden lies with the prosecution. The leading case on the principles to be applied so far as the burden of proof is concerned is *R* v *Hunt* [1987] AC 352. A good recent illustration of these principles applied in a similar statutory context is *Polychronakis* v *Richards, The Independent*, 22 October 1997; *The Times*, 19 November 1997, a case on s. 80(4) and (6) of the Environmental Protection Act 1990.

There is no case law on what is meant by 'reasonable excuse' under this Act. Cases may occur where, because of the complexity of the law, the landlord has misunderstood the position or been badly advised. This may well be accepted. However, where the law is clear but unhelpful (e.g., the requirement to serve notices on a 'building by building' basis), simply taking a chance that there will be no enforcement action cannot be a 'reasonable excuse'.

5.1.3   Offences by officers of a body corporate

Offences by officers of the body corporate are dealt with by s. 10A(3). This can apply to a director, manager, secretary or other similar officer. The offence can be committed by such officers in two alternative ways:

(a)   under s. 10A(3)(a), where the offence by the corporation is committed with the consent or connivance of that officer;

(b)   under s. 10A(3)(b), where the offence is due to neglect by such a person.

There can be joint liability of the company and its officers. Members of the company involved in its management can also be liable for their own acts and defaults (s. 10A(3)).

5.1.4   Prosecution

Offences under s. 10A may be prosecuted by local housing authorities, as defined in s. 1 of the Housing Act 1985 (s. 10A(4)). Prosecutions may also be brought by the police or by way of private prosecution.

5.1.5   Effect of criminal offence on a disposal

Section 10A(5) provides that s. 10A does not affect the validity of a disposal. The expression 'disposal' includes a 'contract to make such a disposal' (see s. 4A(1)(a)). This means that a contract to make a disposal which involves the committing of a criminal offence under s. 10A can be enforced notwithstanding the criminal nature of the disposal.

5.2   METHODS OF AVOIDING THE ACT

5.2.1   Company schemes

The obvious way for a landlord to dispose of property without triggering the 1987 Act is to effect the transaction by means of a company sale. A sale of a company (the main assets of which are flat reversions) is not a disposal within the statute. This loophole was much used as the Act was first drafted. Consequently it was partly closed by the Housing Act 1996, s. 90, which inserted a new paragraph in s. 4(2) of the 1987 Act. A disposal to an associated company is exempt only if it has been an associated company for at least two years (LTA 1987, s. 4(2)(l)). This means that to use company disposals effectively care is needed in devising the company structure which is to be used. A simple route sometimes available is to transfer from the company to an existing holding company all except the property which is intended to be sold by a share transfer.

An example of a complicated company scheme is found in *Michaels* v *Harley House (Marylebone) Ltd, The Times,* 16 March 1997.

5.2.2   Conditional contracts

It has been suggested that conditional contracts can be used to circumvent the 1987 Act. This is not so. A conditional contract is itself a disposal and must be preceded by an appropriate offer to sell to the tenants under s. 5. This being so a contract a condition of which is that the tenants do not exercise their rights is (except in auction contracts) completely pointless, as such a contract can be entered into only after the tenants have declined the right of first refusal. A disposal pursuant to a conditional contract which has not been preceded by s. 5 notices is clearly a criminal offence under s. 10A.

5.2.3   Use of security document

A mortgagee who sells under the statutory power of sale makes a non-exempt disposal (LTA 1987, s. 4(1A)). However, a foreclosure is not a disposal by the mortgagor and nothing in the 1987 Act makes it so. Clearly this possibility must not used in a way which is an abuse of the process of the court within the Rules of the Supreme Court (RSC), Ords 18 and 19(5). In addition, if possession is claimed in the forfeiture proceedings the plaintiff must comply with RSC, Ords 88 or 5(4)(a), which means in effect giving notice to each occupier (*Leicester PBS* v *Shearley* [1951] Ch 90).

5.2.4   Use of s. 18 procedure

This procedure is discussed at 4.12. It may be utilised particularly if the landlord wishes to dispose of an estate which comprises several buildings. Thus, it has been suggested that the s. 18 notice could be served on all the tenants of several buildings on one estate. The difficulty of this is that the disposal which is referred to throughout s. 18 is a disposal under the Act. A notice under s. 18, it will be argued, is clearly intended to be a mirror of the s. 5 notice which would otherwise be used. In considering the proportion of the tenants required to be served or to respond to the notice under s. 18(3), it is hard to escape the conclusion that for the section to make sense in the context of the remainder of the Act this must refer to tenants of one building who could have been validly served with a s. 5 notice. The clinching argument seems to be in the words of s. 18(1)(a), which refer to a s. 18 notice being used where 'any disposal of an estate . . . in . . . the whole or part of a building is proposed to be made by a landlord'. The s. 18 notice which then results, in order to be valid, must be prepared and served on a building-by-building basis. It is quite clear from *Mainwaring* v *Trustees of Henry Smith's Charity* [1996] 2 All ER 220, that the court will guard against s. 18 being used to evade the statutory purpose. This is particularly clear from the comments of Lord Bingham MR, at p. 235:

> the primary purpose of the section ... is to afford protection to the prospective purchaser, and the present situation is not one in which the prospective purchaser has any conceivable need for such protection. That the section 18 procedure is capable of abuse has been demonstrated above.

It cannot be anticipated by a sanguine landlord that s. 18 will be given an interpretation that encourages such abuse. This again strongly suggests that a s. 18 notice must be served on a building-by-building basis.

5.2.5   Structured disposal

It is possible to dispose of a building by a number of transactions none of which in itself is a disposal within the 1987 Act. Disposal of the common parts may not in itself be within the Act. Disposal of a tenancy of a single flat does not come within the Act. Thus if there is a house divided into flats with a garden then the freehold of the garden and a long lease of each flat separately can be disposed of to A Co. Ltd. The freehold that remains can then be disposed of to A Co. Ltd without an offer notice being served as at this stage the freeholder is not a landlord within Part I of the Act. This is because A Co. Ltd is not a qualifying tenant (LTA 1987, s. 3(2)). The qualifying tenants are the tenants in possession of the flats and the freeholder is not their landlord within s. 2(1).

5.2.6   Precarious appurtenances

The tenants are entitled to buy only what the landlord sells. There is no mechanism for including in the sale anything which the landlord does not include in the offer notice. There is scope in this rather obvious fact for a simple mechanism to avoid the 1987 Act. If the landlord offers to sell the reversion to property other than the flats themselves then the Act is inapplicable. The landlord may thus offer to sell the reversion to the flats by a separate contract. There is no obligation to disclose to the tenants that there is to be a simultaneous contract to sell the common parts, e.g., squash courts, swimming pools and golf course or whatever other property is associated with the flats. The efficacy of this route will depend on the nature of the rights which the tenants have in the common parts. Are the rights part of the tenants' leasehold interest? If so this loophole is not available.

5.2.7   Exempt landlords

The various exempt landlords are listed in s. 58. There are two main categories. The first is a variety of public sector landlords including local authorities and most housing associations. There is little scope for making use of these categories to avoid the legislation.

The other category is resident landlords. These are defined in s. 58(2). The exception does not apply to a purpose-built block of flats. This is a building which, as constructed, contains two or more flats (s. 58(3)). If the building is not such a purpose-built block of flats then the landlord is exempt if he or she has occupied a flat in it as his or her only or principal residence for a period of at least the preceding 12 months. This gives some scope for possible abuse.

CHAPTER SIX

Litigation

6.1 INTRODUCTION

There are two venues for litigation under Part I of the LTA 1987. These are the court and the leasehold valuation tribunal. The leasehold valuation tribunal is essentially a rent assessment committee under another name and its procedures are accordingly informal. The crucial difference, however, for the parties between the two forums is the incidence of costs, as to which see below.

6.2 LEASEHOLD VALUATION TRIBUNAL

6.2.1 Jurisdiction

The jurisdiction of the leasehold valuation tribunal is given by s. 13 of the LTA 1987. It is divided into two areas:

(a) any question arising in relation to any matters specified in a notice under section 12A, 12B or 12C, and

(b) any question arising for determination as mentioned in section 8C(4), 12A(5) or 12B(4) . . .

The notices mentioned in s. 13(1)(a) are:

(a) a s. 12A notice, i.e. a notice to a purchaser under which the tenants elect to take the benefit of that purchaser's contract (see Form 19, Appendix B);

(b) a s. 12B notice, i.e. a notice by qualifying tenants to compel sale by a purchaser (see Form 20, Appendix B);

(c) a s. 12C notice, i.e. a notice by qualifying tenants to compel the grant of a new lease where there has been a surrender by the landlord.

The questions arising for determination in ss. 8C(4), 12A(5) or 12B(4) mentioned in s. 13(1)(b) are briefly:

(a) under s. 8C(4) an application to the tribunal to determine the value of a consideration which was not a money consideration (see 2.9);

(b) under s. 12A(5), an application to determine the subject matter and terms on which the tenant may take the benefit of a contract when the building in question has been disposed of together with other property (see 4.6);

(c) under s. 12B(4) an application to determine the subject matter and terms on which the tenants may take the benefit of a disposal where the disposal included other property (see 4.7.1).

6.2.2   Leasehold valuation tribunal described

The leasehold valuation tribunal is in fact a rent assessment committee by another name. This is provided for by s. 52A of the LTA 1987. Rent assessment committees are constituted under Sch. 10 of the Rent Act 1977.

Section 52A of the LTA 1987 provides for rules to be made or forms prescribed. The current rules applicable are the Rent Assessment Committee (England and Wales) (Leasehold Valuation Tribunal) Regulations 1993 (SI 1993 No. 2408). These are amended by the following statutory instruments: the Rent Assessment Committee (England and Wales) (Leasehold Valuation Tribunal) (Amendment) Regulations 1996 (SI 1996 No. 2305); the Housing Act 1996 (Consequential Amendments) Order 1997 (SI 1997 No. 64); the Rent Assessment Committee (England and Wales) (Leasehold Valuation Tribunal) (Amendment) Regulations 1997 (SI 1997 No. 1854).

6.2.3   Procedure for application

There is no prescribed form to be used in the application to the tribunal. The information to be used is contained in an application set out in Sch. 1 to the 1993 Regulations (as amended). The application can be simply drafted in numbered paragraphs following the format of Sch. 1.

There is no fee payable for an application under s. 13 of the LTA 1987.

There is no right of appeal to the High Court from the rent assessment committee on an application under s. 13. Instead a right of appeal is given to the Lands Tribunal (LTA 1987, s. 52A). The appeal is governed by the Housing Act 1980, Sch. 2, para. 2. This provides that the persons who may appeal are 'any person who— (a) appears before a tribunal in proceedings to which he was a part; and (b) is dissatisfied with its decision'.

6.2.4   Costs in the leasehold valuation tribunal

There are no costs orders made by the leasehold valuation tribunal. Section 52A of the LTA 1987 provides specifically that each party to an application shall bear its own costs.

On an appeal to the Lands Tribunal there is a risk of costs. Costs orders are in the discretion of the court (Lands Tribunal Rules 1996 (SI 1996 No. 1021)) and follow High Court and county court principles.

In reality the procedure both in the leasehold valuation tribunal and on appeal is expensive. Litigants in person are likely to find the law and procedures bewildering. Landlords take advantage of expert legal advice and bewildering company structures to confuse tenants. In consequence the tenant also needs expert assistance. This legislation, as with other reforms, does not give the tenant the cost-effective solutions that are desirable. Removing the avenue of automatic right of appeal to the Lands Tribunal would probably be beneficial as it seems that landlords are able to use the threat of appeal to the Lands Tribunal to bring pressure to bear on the tenants.

6.3   APPLICATIONS TO THE COURT

Section 60(1) of the LTA 1987 provides that 'the court' refers either to the county court or to the High Court.

A specific procedure for enforcement of obligations under s. 19 of the Act is laid down in the County Court Rules (CCR), Ord. 43. (This order is re-enacted in the Civil Procedure Rules 1998.)

6.3.1   County court jurisdiction

County court jurisdiction is conferred by s. 52 of the LTA 1987. The county court can deal with any question which is not within the jurisdiction of the leasehold valuation tribunal under s. 13.

6.3.2 Special jurisdiction procedure

The court is given a special jurisdiction in the enforcement of the obligations imposed by Part I of the LTA 1987 by s. 19 of the Act. The court is given the power, on the application of 'any person interested', to make an order requiring any default in complying with such a duty to be made good within a specified time.

Proceedings cannot be taken under s. 19 unless a notice has been served on the person in default requiring him to make good the default. Proceedings can then be started once 14 days have elapsed from the default notice without the person in default complying.

6.3.3 Order 43

The CCR, Ord. 43, r. 2 requires the proceedings to be commenced by originating application and the respondent to file an answer (Ord. 43, r. 2(2)).

Order 43, r. 17 contains requirements for the originating application. The notice served under s. 19(2)(a) of the 1987 Act must be appended to the originating application and a further copy of the notice filed.

6.3.4 The High Court

Proceedings in the High Court are governed by RSC Ord. 97. (This order is re-enacted in the Civil Procedure Rules 1998.) Proceedings are assigned to the Chancery Division and commenced by originating summons. The summons may be issued in the district registry to which the claim relates or in Chancery Chambers.

If the application is for enforcement of obligations under s. 19 of the 1987 Act then a copy of the notice served under s. 19(2)(a) must be attached to the originating summons and a further copy of the notice filed (RSC Ord. 97, r. 14).

Service of any notice in the proceedings is in accordance with s. 54 of the 1987 Act, and if on the landlord at the address given in compliance with s. 48 of that Act (RSC Ord. 97, r. 18).

Landlord and Tenant Act 1987

LANDLORD AND TENANT ACT 1987
PART I
TENANTS' RIGHTS OF FIRST REFUSAL
Preliminary

1. Qualifying tenants to have rights of first refusal on disposals by landlord

(1) A landlord shall not make a relevant disposal affecting any premises to which at the time of the disposal this Part applies unless—

(a) he has in accordance with section 5 previously served a notice under that section with respect to the disposal on the qualifying tenants of the flats contained in those premises (being a notice by virtue of which rights of first refusal are conferred on those tenants); and

(b) the disposal is made in accordance with the requirements of sections 6 to 10.

(2) Subject to subsections (3) and (4), this Part applies to premises if—

(a) they consist of the whole or part of a building; and

(b) they contain two or more flats held by qualifying tenants; and

(c) the number of flats held by such tenants exceeds 50 per cent of the total number of flats contained in the premises.

(3) This Part does not apply to premises falling within subsection (2) if—

(a) any part or parts of the premises is or are occupied or intended to be occupied otherwise than for residential purposes; and

(b)   the internal floor area of that part or those parts (taken together) exceeds 50 per cent of the internal floor area of the premises (taken as a whole);

and for the purposes of this subsection the internal floor area of any common parts shall be disregarded.

(4)   This Part also does not apply to any such premises at a time when the interest of the landlord in the premises is held by an exempt landlord or a resident landlord.

(5)   The Secretary of State may by order substitute for the percentage for the time being specified in subsection (3)(b) such other percentage as is specified in the order.

2.   Landlords for the purposes of Part I

(1)   Subject to subsection (2) and section 4(1A) a person is for the purposes of this Part the landlord in relation to any premises consisting of the whole or part of a building if he is—

(a)   the immediate landlord of the qualifying tenants of the flats contained in those premises, or

(b)   where any of those tenants is a statutory tenant, the person who, apart from the statutory tenancy, would be entitled to possession of the flat in question.

(2)   Where the person who is, in accordance with subsection (1), the landlord in relation to any such premises for the purposes of this Part ('the immediate landlord') is himself a tenant of those premises under a tenancy which is either—

(a)   a tenancy for a term of less than seven years, or

(b)   a tenancy for a longer term but terminable within the first seven years at the option of the person who is the landlord under that tenancy ('the superior landlord'),

the superior landlord shall also be regarded as the landlord in relation to those premises for the purposes of this Part and, if the superior landlord is himself a tenant of those premises under a tenancy falling within paragraph (a) or (b) above, the person who is the landlord under the tenancy shall also be so regarded (and so on).

3.   Qualifying tenants

(1)   Subject to the following provisions of this section, a person is for the purposes of this Part a qualifying tenant of a flat if he is the tenant of the flat under a tenancy other than—

(a)   a protected shorthold tenancy as defined in section 52 of the Housing Act 1980;

(b)   a tenancy to which Part II of the Landlord and Tenant Act 1954 (business tenancies) applies;

(c)   a tenancy terminable on the cessation of his employment; or

(d)   an assured tenancy or assured agricultural occupancy within the meaning of Part I of the Housing Act 1988.

(2)   A person is not to be regarded as being a qualifying tenant of any flat contained in any particular premises consisting of the whole or part of a building if—

by virtue of one or more tenancies none of which falls within paragraphs (a) to (d) of subsection (1), he is the tenant not only of the flat in question but also of at least two other flats contained in those premises.

(3)   For the purposes of subsection (2) any tenant of a flat contained in the premises in question who is a body corporate shall be treated as the tenant of any other flat so contained and let to an associated company.

(4)   A tenant of a flat whose landlord is a qualifying tenant of that flat is not to be regarded as being a qualifying tenant of that flat.

4. Relevant disposals

(1)   In this Part references to a relevant disposal affecting any premises to which this Part applies are references to the disposal by the landlord of any estate or interest (whether legal or equitable) in any such premises, including the disposal of any such estate or interest in any common parts of any such premises but excluding—

(a)   the grant of any tenancy under which the demised premises consist of a single flat (whether with or without any appurtenant premises); and

(b)   any of the disposals falling within subsection (2).

(1A)   Where an estate or interest of the landlord has been mortgaged, the reference in subsection (1) above to the disposal of an estate or interest by the landlord includes a reference to its disposal by the mortgagee in exercise of a power of sale or leasing, whether or not the disposal is made in the name of the landlord; and, in relation to such a proposed disposal by the mortgagee, any reference in the following provisions of this Part to the landlord shall be construed as a reference to the mortgagee.

(2)   The disposals referred to in subsection (1)(b) are—

(a)   a disposal of—

(i)   any interest of a beneficiary in settled land within the meaning of the Settled Land Act 1925,

(ii)   . . .

(iii)   any incorporeal hereditament;

(aa)   a disposal by way of security for a loan;

(b)   a disposal to a trustee in bankruptcy or to the liquidator of a company;

(c) a disposal in pursuance of an order made under—

(i) section 23A or 24 of the Matrimonial Causes Act 1973 (property adjustment orders in connection with matrimonial proceedings),

(ii) section 24A of the Matrimonial Causes Act 1973 (orders for the sale of property in connection with matrimonial proceedings) where the order includes provision requiring the property concerned to be offered for sale to a person or class of persons specified in the order,

(iii) section 2 of the Inheritance (Provision for Family and Dependants) Act 1975 (orders as to financial provision to be made from estate),

(iv) section 17(1) of the Matrimonial and Family Proceedings Act 1984 (property adjustment orders after overseas divorce, etc.),

(v) section 17(2) of the Matrimonial and Family Proceedings Act 1984 (orders for the sale of property after overseas divorce, etc.) where the order includes provision requiring the property concerned to be offered for sale to a person or class of persons specified in the order, or

(vi) paragraph 1 of Schedule 1 to the Children Act 1989 (orders for financial relief against parents);

(d) a disposal in pursuance of a compulsory purchase order or in pursuance of an agreement entered into in circumstances where, but for the agreement, such an order would have been made or (as the case may be) carried into effect;

(da) a disposal of any freehold or leasehold interest in pursuance of Chapter I of Part I of the Leasehold Reform, Housing and Urban Development Act 1993;

(e) a disposal by way of gift to a member of the landlord's family or to a charity;

(f) a disposal by one charity to another of an estate or interest in land which prior to the disposal is functional land of the first-mentioned charity and which is intended to be functional land of the other charity once the disposal is made;

(g) a disposal consisting of the transfer of an estate or interest held on trust for any person where the disposal is made in connection with the appointment of a new trustee or in connection with the discharge of any trustee;

(h) a disposal consisting of a transfer by two or more persons who are members of the same family either—

(i) to fewer of their number, or

(ii) to a different combination of members of the family (but one that includes at least one of the transferors);

(i) a disposal in pursuance of a contract, option or right of pre-emption binding on the landlord (except as provided by section 8D (application of sections 11 to 17 to disposal in pursuance of option or right of pre-emption));

(j) a disposal consisting of the surrender of a tenancy in pursuance of any covenant, condition or agreement contained in it;

(k) a disposal to the Crown; and

(l) a disposal by a body corporate to a company which has been an associated company of that body for at least two years.

(3) In this part 'disposal' means a disposal whether by the creation or the transfer of an estate or interest and—

(a) includes the surrender of a tenancy and the grant of an option or right of pre-emption, but

(b) excludes a disposal under the terms of a will or under the law relating to intestacy;

and references in this Part to the transferee in connection with a disposal shall be construed accordingly.

(4) In this section 'appurtenant premises', in relation to any flat, means any yard, garden, outhouse or appurtenance (not being a common part of the building containing the flat) which belongs to, or is usually enjoyed with, the flat.

(5) A person is a member of another's family for the purposes of this section if—

(a) that person is the spouse of that other person, or the two of them live together as husband and wife, or

(b) that person is that other person's parent, grandparent, child, grandchild, brother, sister, uncle, aunt, nephew or niece.

(6) For the purposes of subsection (5)(b)—

(a) a relationship by marriage shall be treated as a relationship by blood,

(b) a relationship of the half-blood shall be treated as a relationship of the whole blood,

(c) the stepchild of a person shall be treated as his child, and

(d) an illegitimate child shall be treated as the legitimate child of his mother and reputed father.

4A. Application of provisions to contracts

(1) The provisions of this Part apply to a contract to create or transfer an estate or interest in land, whether conditional or unconditional and whether or not enforceable by specific performance, as they apply in relation to a disposal consisting of the creation or transfer of such an estate or interest.

As they so apply—

(a)   references to a disposal of any description shall be construed as references to a contract to make such a disposal;

(b)   references to making a disposal of any description shall be construed as references to entering into a contract to make such a disposal; and

(c)   references to the transferee under the disposal shall be construed as references to the other party to the contract and include a reference to any other party to whom an estate or interest is to be granted or transferred in pursuance of the contract.

(2)   The provisions of this Part apply to an assignment of rights under such a contract as is mentioned in subsection (1) as they apply in relation to a disposal consisting of the transfer of an estate or interest in land.

As they so apply—

(a)   references to a disposal of any description shall be construed as references to an assignment of rights under a contract to make such a disposal;

(b)   references to making a disposal of any description shall be construed as references to making an assignment of rights under a contract to make such a disposal;

(c)   references to the landlord shall be construed as reference to the assignor; and

(d)   references to the transferee under the disposal shall be construed as references to the assignee of such rights.

(3)   The provisions of this Part apply to a contract to make such an assignment as is mentioned in subsection (2) as they apply (in accordance with subsection (1)) to a contract to create or transfer an estate or interest in land.

(4)   Nothing in this section affects the operation of the provisions of this Part relating to options or rights of pre-emption.

Rights of first refusal

5.   Landlord required to serve offer notice on tenants

(1)   Where the landlord proposes to make a relevant disposal affecting premises to which this Part applies, he shall serve a notice under this section (an 'offer notice') on the qualifying tenants of the flats contained in the premises (the 'constituent flats').

(2)   An offer notice must comply with the requirements of whichever is applicable of the following sections—

section 5A (requirements in case of contract to be completed by conveyance, etc.,

section 5B (requirements in case of sale at auction),

section 5C (requirements in case of grant of option or right of pre-emption),

section 5D (requirements in case of conveyance not preceded by contract, etc.);

and in the case of a disposal to which section 5E applies (disposal for non-monetary consideration) shall also comply with the requirements of that section.

(3)   Where a landlord proposes to effect a transaction involving the disposal of an estate or interest in more than one building (whether or not involving the same estate or interest), he shall, for the purpose of complying with this section, sever the transaction so as to deal with each building separately.

(4)   If, as a result of the offer notice being served on different tenants on different dates, the period specified in the notice as the period for accepting the offer would end on different dates, the notice shall have effect in relation to all the qualifying tenants on whom it is served as if it provided for the period to end with the latest of those dates.

(5)   A landlord who has not served an offer notice on all of the qualifying tenants on whom it was required to be served shall nevertheless be treated as having complied with this section—

(a)   if he has served an offer notice on not less than 90% of the qualifying tenants on whom such a notice was required to be served, or

(b)   where the qualifying tenants on whom it was required to be served number less than ten, if he has served such a notice on all but one of them.

5A.   Offer notice: requirements in case of contract to be completed by conveyance, etc.

(1)   The following requirements must be met in relation to an offer notice where the disposal consists of entering into a contract to create or transfer an estate or interest in land.

(2)   The notice must contain particulars of the principle terms of the disposal proposed by the landlord, including in particular—

(a)   the property, and the estate or interest in that property, to which the contract relates,

(b)   the principal terms of the contract (including the deposit and consideration required).

(3)   The notice must state that the notice constitutes an offer by the landlord to enter into a contract on those terms which may be accepted by the requisite majority of qualifying tenants of the constituent flats.

(4)   The notice must specify a period within which that offer may be so accepted, being a period of not less than two months which is to begin with the date of service of the notice.

(5)   The notice must specify a further period of not less than two months within which a person or persons may be nominated by the tenants under section 6.

(6)   This section does not apply to the grant of an option or right of pre-emption (see section 5C).

5B.   Offer notice: requirements in case of sale by auction

(1)   The following requirements must be met in relation to an offer notice where the landlord proposes to make the disposal by means of a sale at a public auction held in England and Wales.

(2)   The notice must contain particulars of the principal terms of the disposal proposed by the landlord, including in particular the property to which it relates and the estate or interest in that property proposed to be disposed of.

(3)   The notice must state that the disposal is proposed to be made by means of a sale at a public auction.

(4)   The notice must state that the notice constitutes an offer by the landlord, which may be accepted by the requisite majority of qualifying tenants of the constituent flats, for the contract (if any) entered into by the landlord at the auction to have effect as if a person or persons nominated by them, and not the purchaser, had entered into it.

(5)   The notice must specify a period within which that offer may be so accepted, being a period of not less than two months beginning with the date of service of the notice.

(6)   The notice must specify a further period of not less than 28 days within which a person or persons may be nominated by the tenants under section 6.

(7)   The notice must be served not less than four months or more than six months before the date of the auction; and—

(a)   the period specified in the notice as the period within which the offer may be accepted must end not less than two months before the date of the auction, and

(b)   the period specified in the notice as the period within which a person may be nominated under section 6 must end not less than 28 days before the date of the auction.

(8)   Unless the time and place of the auction and the name of the auctioneers are stated in the notice, the landlord shall, not less than 28 days before the date of the auction, serve on the requisite majority of qualifying tenants of the constituent flats a further notice stating those particulars.

5C. Offer notice: requirements in case of grant or option or right of pre-emption

(1) The following requirements must be met in relation to an offer notice where the disposal consists of the grant of an option or right of pre-emption.

(2) The notice must contain particulars of the principal terms of the disposal proposed by the landlord, including in particular—

(a) the property, and the estate or interest in that property, to which the option or right of pre-emption relates,

(b) the consideration required by the landlord for granting the option or right of pre-emption, and

(c) the principal terms on which the option or right of pre-emption would be exercisable, including the consideration payable on its exercise.

(3) The notice must state that the notice constitutes an offer by the landlord to grant an option or right of pre-emption on those terms which may be accepted by the requisite majority of qualifying tenants of the constituent flats.

(4) The notice must specify a period within which that offer may be so accepted, being a period of not less than two months which is to begin with the date of service of the notice.

(5) The notice must specify a further period of not less than two months within which a person or persons may be nominated by the tenants under section 6.

5D. Offer notice: requirements in case of conveyance not preceded by contract, etc.

(1) The following requirements must be met in relation to an offer notice where the disposal is not made in pursuance of a contract, option or right of pre-emption binding on the landlord.

(2) The notice must contain particulars of the principal terms of the disposal proposed by the landlord, including in particular—

(a) the property to which it relates and the estate or interest in that property proposed to be disposed of, and

(b) the consideration required by the landlord for making the disposal.

(3) The notice must state that the notice constitutes an offer by the landlord to dispose of the property on those terms which may be accepted by the requisite majority of qualifying tenants of the constituent flats.

(4) The notice must specify a period within which that offer may be so accepted, being a period of not less than two months which is to begin with the date of service of the notice.

(5)   The notice must specify a further period of not less than two months within which a person or persons may be nominated by the tenants under section 6.

5E.   Offer notice: disposal for non-monetary consideration

(1)   This section applies where, in any case to which section 5 applies, the consideration required by the landlord for making the disposal does not consist, or does not wholly consist, or money.

(2)   The offer notice, in addition to complying with whichever is applicable of sections 5A to 5D, must state—

(a)   that an election may made under section 8C (explaining its effect), and

(b)   that, accordingly, the notice also constitutes an offer by the landlord, which may be accepted by the requisite majority of qualifying tenants of the constituent flats, for a person or persons nominated by them to acquire the property in pursuance of sections 11 to 17.

(3)   The notice must specify a period within which that offer may be so accepted, being a period of not less than two months which is to begin with the date of service of the notice.

6.   Acceptance of landlord's offer: general provisions

(1)   Where a landlord has served an offer notice, he shall not during—

(a)   the period specified in the notice as the period during which the offer may be accepted, or

(b)   such longer period as may be agreed between him and the requisite majority of the qualifying tenants of the constituent flats,

dispose of the protected interest except to a person or persons nominated by the tenants under this section

(2)   Where an acceptance notice is duly served on him, he shall not during the protected period (see subsection (4) below) dispose of the protected interest except to a person duly nominated for the purposes of this section by the requisite majority of qualifying tenants of the constituent flats (a 'nominated person').

(3)   An 'acceptance notice' means a notice served on the landlord by the requisite majority of qualifying tenants of the constituent flats informing him that the persons by whom it is served accept the offer contained in his notice.

An acceptance notice is 'duly served' if it is served within—

(a)   the period specified in the offer notice as the period within which the offer may be accepted, or

(b)   such longer period as may be agreed between the landlord and the requisite majority of qualifying tenants of the constituent flats.

(4)   The 'protected period' is the period beginning with the date of service of the acceptance notice and ending with—

(a) the end of the period specified in the offer notice as the period for nominating a person under this section, or

(b) such later date as may be agreed between the landlord and the requisite majority of qualifying tenants of the constituent flats.

(5) A person is 'duly nominated' for the purposes of this section if he is nominated at the same time as the acceptance notice is served or at any time after that notice is served and before the end of—

(a) the period specified in the offer notice as the period for nomination, or

(b) such longer period as may be agreed between the landlord and the requisite majority of qualifying tenants of the constituent flats.

(6) A person nominated for the purposes of this section by the requisite majority of qualifying tenants of the constituent flats may be replaced by another person so nominated if, and only if, he has (for any reason) ceased to be able to act as a nominated person.

(7) Where two or more persons have been nominated and any of them ceases to act without being replaced, the remaining person or persons so nominated may continue to act.

7. Failure to accept landlord's offer or to make nomination

(1) Where a landlord has served an offer notice on the qualifying tenants of the constituent flats and—

(a) no acceptance notice is duly served on the landlord, or

(b) no person is nominated for the purposes of section 6 during the protected period,

the landlord may, during the period of 12 months beginning with the end of that period, dispose of the protected interest to such person as he thinks fit, but subject to the following restrictions.

(2) Where the offer notice was one to which section 5B applied (sale by auction), the restrictions are—

(a) that the disposal is made by means of a sale at a public auction, and

(b) that the other terms correspond to those specified in the offer notice.

(3) In any other case the restrictions are—

(a) that the deposit and consideration required are not less than those specified in the offer notice, and

(b) that the other terms correspond to those specified in the offer notice.

(4) The entitlement of a landlord, by virtue of this section or any other corresponding provision of this Part, to dispose of the protected interest during a specified period of 12 months extends only to a disposal of that

interest, and accordingly the requirements of section 1(1) must be satisfied with respect to any other disposal by him during that period of 12 months (unless the disposal is not a relevant disposal affecting any premises to which at the time of the disposal this Part applies).

8. Landlord's obligations in case of acceptance and nomination

(1) This section applies where a landlord serves an offer notice on the qualifying tenants of the constituent flat and—

(a) an acceptance notice is duly served on him, and

(b) a person is duly nominated for the purposes of section 6,

by the requisite majority of qualifying tenants of the constituent flats.

(2) Subject to the following provisions of this Part, the landlord shall not dispose of the protected interest except to the nominated person.

(3) The landlord shall, within the period of one month beginning with the date of service of notice of nomination, either—

(a) serve notice on the nominated person indicating an intention no longer to proceed with the disposal of the protected interest, or

(b) be obliged to proceed in accordance with the following provisions of this Part,

(4) A notice under subsection (3)(a) is a notice of withdrawal for the purposes of section 9B(2) to (4) (consequences of notice of withdrawal by landlord).

(5) Nothing in this section shall be taken as prejudicing the application of the provisions of this Part to any further offer notice served by the landlord on the qualifying tenants of the constituent flats.

8A. Landlord's obligation: general provisions

(1) This section applies where the landlord is obliged to proceed and the offer notice was not one to which section 5B applied (sale by auction).

(2) The landlord shall, within the period of one month beginning with the date of service of the notice of nomination, send to the nominated person a form of contract for the acquisition of the protected interest on the terms specified in the landlord's offer notice.

(3) If he fails to do so, the following provisions of this Part apply as if he had given notice under section 9B (notice of withdrawal by landlord) at the end of that period.

(4) If the landlord complies with subsection (2), the nominated person shall, within the period of two months beginning with the date on which it is sent or such longer period beginning with that date as may be agreed between the landlord and that person, either—

(a) serve notice on the landlord indicating an intention no longer to proceed with the acquisition of the protected interest, or

(b)   offer an exchange of contracts, that is to say, sign the contract and send it to the landlord, together with the requisite deposit.

In this subsection 'the requisite deposit' means a deposit of an amount determined by or under the contract or an amount equal to 10 per cent of the consideration, whichever is the less.

(5)   If the nominated person—

(a)   serves notice in pursuance of paragraph (a) of subsection (4), or

(b)   fails to offer an exchange of contracts within the period specified in that subsection,

the following provisions of this Part apply as if he had given notice under section 9A (withdrawal by nominated person) at the same time as that notice or, as the case may be, at the end of that period.

(6)   If the nominated person offers an exchange of contracts within the period specified in subsection (4), but the landlord fails to complete the exchange within the period of seven days beginning with the day on which he received that person's contract, the following provisions of this Part apply as if the landlord had given notice under section 9B (withdrawal by landlord) at the end of that period.

8B.   Landlord's obligation: election in case of sale at auction

(1)   This section applies where the landlord is obliged to proceed and the offer notice was one to which section 5B applied (sale by auction).

(2)   The nominated person may, by notice served on the landlord not less than 28 days before the date of the auction, elect that the provisions of this section shall apply.

(3)   If a contract for the disposal is entered into at the auction, the landlord shall, within the period of seven days beginning with the date of the auction, send a copy of the contract to the nominated person.

(4)   If, within the period of 28 days beginning with the date on which such a copy is so sent, the nominated person—

(a)   serves notice on the landlord accepting the terms of the contract, and

(b)   fulfils any conditions falling to be fulfilled by the purchaser on entering into the contract,

the contract shall have effect as if the nominated person, and not the purchaser, had entered into the contract.

(5)   Unless otherwise agreed, any time limit in the contract as it has effect by virtue of subsection (4) shall start to run again on the service of notice under that subsection; and nothing in the contract as it has effect by virtue of a notice under this section shall require the nominated person to complete the purchase before the end of the period of 28 days beginning with the day on which he is deemed to have entered into the contract.

(6)   If the nominated person—

(a)   does not serve notice on the landlord under subsection (2) by the time mentioned in that subsection, or

(b)   does not satisfy the requirements of subsection (4) within the period mentioned in that subsection,

the following provisions of this Part apply as if he had given notice under section 9A (withdrawal by nominated person) at the end of that period.

8C.   Election in case of disposal for non-monetary consideration

(1)   This section applies where an acceptance notice is duly served on the landlord indicating an intention to accept the offer referred to in section 5E (offer notice: disposal for non-monetary consideration).

(2)   The requisite majority of qualifying tenants of the constituent flats may, by notice served on the landlord within—

(a)   the period specified in the offer notice for nominating a person or persons for the purposes of section 6, and

(b)   such longer period as may be agreed between the landlord and the requisite majority of qualifying tenants of the constituent flats,

elect that the following provisions shall apply.

(3)   Where such an election is made and the landlord disposes of the protected interest on terms corresponding to those specified in his offer notice in accordance with section 5A, 5B, 5C or 5D, sections 11 to 17 shall have effect as if—

(a)   no notice under section 5 had been served;

(b)   in section 11A(3) (period for serving notice requiring information, etc.), the reference to four months were a reference to 28 days; and

(c)   in section 12A(2) and 12B(3) (period for exercise of tenants' rights against purchaser) each reference to six months were a reference to two months.

(4)   For the purposes of sections 11 to 17 as they have effect by virtue of subsection (3) so much of the consideration for the original disposal as did not consist of money shall be treated as such amount in money as was equivalent to its value in the hands of the landlord.

The landlord or the nominated person may apply to have that amount determined by a leasehold valuation tribunal.

8D.   Disposal in pursuance of option or right of pre-emption

(1)   Where—

(a)   the original disposal was the grant of an option or right of pre-emption, and

(b)   in pursuance of the option or right, the landlord makes another disposal affecting the premises ('the later disposal') before the end of the period specified in subsection (2), sections 11 to 17 shall have effect as if the later disposal, and not the original disposal, were the relevant disposal.

(2)   The period referred to in subsection (1)(b) is the period of four months beginning with the date by which—

(a)   notices under section 3A of the Landlord and Tenant Act 1985 (duty of new landlord to inform tenants of rights) relating to the original disposal, or

(b)   where that section does not apply, documents of any other description—

(i)   indicating that the original disposal has taken place, and

(ii)   alerting the tenants to the existence of their rights under this Part and the time within which any such rights must be exercised,

have been served on the requisite majority of qualifying tenants of the constituent flats.

8E.   Covenant, etc. affecting landlord's power to dispose

(1)   Where the landlord is obliged to proceed but is precluded by a covenant, condition or other obligation from disposing of the protected interest to the nominated person unless the consent of some other person is obtained—

(a)   he shall use his best endeavours to secure that the consent of that person to that disposal is given, and

(b)   if it appears to him that that person is obliged not to withhold his consent unreasonably but has nevertheless so withheld it, he shall institute proceedings for a declaration to that effect.

(2)   Subsection (1) ceases to apply if a notice of withdrawal is served under section 9A or 9B (withdrawal of either party from transaction) or if notice is served under section 10 (lapse of landlord's offer: premises ceasing to be premises to which this Part applies).

(3)   Where the landlord has discharged any duty imposed on him by subsection (1) but any such consent as is there mentioned has been withheld, and no such declaration as is there mentioned has been made, the landlord may serve a notice on the nominated person stating that to be the case.

When such a notice has been served, the landlord may, during the period of 12 months beginning with the date of service of the notice, dispose of the protected interest to such person as he thinks fit, but subject to the following restrictions.

(4)   Where the offer notice was one to which section 5B applied (sale by auction), the restrictions are—

(a)   that the disposal is made by means of a sale at a public auction, and

(b) that the other terms correspond to those specified in the offer notice.

(5) In any other case the restrictions are—

(a) that the deposit and consideration required are not less than those specified in the offer notice or, if higher, those agreed between the landlord and the nominated person (subject to contract), and

(b) that the other terms correspond to those specified in the offer notice.

(6) Where notice is given under subsection (3), the landlord may recover from the nominated party and the qualifying tenants who served the acceptance notice any costs reasonably incurred by him in connection with the disposal between the end of the first four weeks of the nomination period and the time when that notice is served by him.

Any such liability of the nominated person and those tenants is a joint and several liability.

9A.   Notice of withdrawal by nominated person

(1) Where the landlord is obliged to proceed, the nominated person may serve notice on the landlord (a 'notice of withdrawal') indicating his intention no longer to proceed with the acquisition of the protected interest.

(2) If at any time the nominated person becomes aware that the number of the qualifying tenants of the constituent flats desiring to proceed with the acquisition of the protected interest is less than the requisite majority of qualifying tenants of those flats, he shall forthwith serve a notice of withdrawal.

(3) Where notice of withdrawal is given by the nominated person under this section, the landlord may, during the period of 12 months beginning with the date of service of the notice, dispose of the protected interest to such person as he thinks fit, but subject to the following restrictions.

(4) Where the offer notice was one to which section 5B applied (sale by auction), the restrictions are—

(a) that the disposal is made by means of a sale at a public auction, and

(b) that the other terms correspond to those specified in the offer notice.

(5) In any other case the restrictions are—

(a) that the deposit and consideration required are not less than those specified in the offer notice or, if higher, those agreed between the landlord and the nominated person (subject to contract), and

(b) that the other terms correspond to those specified in the offer notice.

(6)   If notice of withdrawal is served under this section before the end of the first four weeks of the nomination period specified in the offer notice, the nominated person and the qualifying tenants who served the acceptance notice are not liable for any costs incurred by the landlord in connection with the disposal.

(7)   If notice of withdrawal is served under this section after the end of those four weeks, the landlord may recover from the nominated person and the qualifying tenants who served the acceptance notice any costs reasonably incurred by him in connection with the disposal between the end of those four weeks and the time when the notice of withdrawal was served on him.

Any such liability of the nominated person and those tenants is a joint and several liability.

(8)   This section does not apply after a binding contract for the disposal of the protected interest—

(a)   has been entered into by the landlord and the nominated person, or

(b)   has otherwise come into existence between the landlord and the nominated person by virtue of any provision of this Part.

9B.   Notice of withdrawal by landlord

(1)   Where the landlord is obliged to proceed, he may serve notice on the nominated person (a 'notice of withdrawal') indicating his intention no longer to proceed with the disposal of the protected interest.

(2)   Where a notice of withdrawal is given by the landlord, he is not entitled to dispose of the protected interest during the period of 12 months beginning with the date of service of the notice.

(3)   If a notice of withdrawal is served before the end of the first four weeks of the nomination period specified in the offer notice, the landlord is not liable for any costs incurred in connection with the disposal by the nominated person and the qualifying tenants who served the acceptance notice.

(4)   If a notice of withdrawal is served after the end of those four weeks, the nominated person and the qualifying tenants who served the acceptance notice may recover from the landlord any costs reasonably incurred by them in connection with the disposal between the end of those four weeks and the time when the notice of withdrawal was served.

(5)   This section does not apply after a binding contract for the disposal of the protected interest—

(a)   has been entered into by the landlord and the nominated person, or

(b)   has otherwise come into existence between the landlord and the nominated person by virtue of any provision of this Part.

10.   Lapse of landlord's offer

(1)   If after a landlord has served an offer notice the premises concerned cease to be premises to which this Part applies, the landlord may serve a notice on the qualifying tenants of the constituent flats stating—

(a)   that the premises have ceased to be premises to which this Part applies, and

(b)   that the offer notice, and anything done in pursuance of it, is to be treated as not having been served or done;
and on the service of such a notice the provisions of this Part cease to have effect in relation to that disposal.

(2)   A landlord who has not served such a notice on all of the qualifying tenants of the constituent flats shall nevertheless be treated as having duly served a notice under subsection (1)—

(a)   if he has served such a notice on not less than 90% of those tenants, or

(b)   where those qualifying tenants number less than ten, if he has served such a notice on all but one of them.

(3)   Where the landlord is entitled to serve a notice under subsection (1) but does not do so, this Part shall continue to have effect in relation to the disposal in question as if the premises in question were still premises to which this Part applies.

(4)   The above provisions of this section do not apply after a binding contract for the disposal of the protected interest—

(a)   has been entered into by the landlord and the nominated person, or

(b)   has otherwise come into existence between the landlord and the nominated person by virtue of any provision of this Part.

(5)   Where a binding contract for the disposal of the protected interest has been entered into between the landlord and the nominated person but it has been lawfully rescinded by the landlord, the landlord may, during the period of 12 months beginning with the date of the rescission of the contract, dispose of that interest to such person (and on such terms) as he thinks fit.

10A.   Offence of failure to comply with requirements of Part I

(1)   A landlord commits an offence if, without reasonable excuse, he makes a relevant disposal affecting premises to which this Part applies—

(a)   without having first complied with the requirements of section 5 as regards the service of notices on the qualifying tenants of flats contained in the premises, or

(b)   in contravention of any prohibition or restriction imposed by sections 6 to 10.

(2) A person guilty of an offence under this section is liable on summary conviction to a fine not exceeding level 5 on the standard scale.

(3) Where an offence under this section committed by a body corporate is proved—

(a) to have committed with the consent or connivance of a director, manager, secretary or other similar officer of the body corporate, or a person purporting to act in such capacity, or

(b) to be due to any neglect on the part of such an officer or person, he, as well as the body corporate, is guilty of the offence and liable to be proceeded against and punished accordingly.

Where the affairs of a body corporate are managed by its members, the above provision applies in relation to the acts and defaults of a member in connection with his functions of management as if he were a director of the body corporate.

(4) Proceedings for an offence under this section may be brought by a local housing authority (within the meaning of section 1 of the Housing Act 1985).

(5) Nothing in this section affects the validity of the disposal.

Enforcement by tenants of rights against purchaser

11. Circumstances in which tenants' rights enforceable against purchaser

(1) The following provisions of this Part apply where a landlord has made a relevant disposal affecting premises to which at the time of the disposal this Part applied ('the original disposal'), and either—

(a) no notice was served by the landlord under section 5 with respect to that disposal, or

(b) the disposal was made in contravention of any provision of sections 6 to 10,

and the premises are still premises to which this Part applies.

(2) In those circumstances the requisite majority of the qualifying tenants of the flats contained in the premises affected by the relevant disposal (the 'constituent flats') have the rights conferred by the following provisions—

section 11A (right to information as to terms of disposal, etc.),

section 12A (right of qualifying tenants to take benefit of contract),

section 12B (right of qualifying tenants to compel sale, etc. by purchaser), and

section 12C (right of qualifying tenants to compel grant of new tenancy by superior landlord),

(3) In those sections the transferee under the original disposal (or, in the case of the surrender of a tenancy, the superior landlord) is referred to as 'the purchaser'.

This shall not be read as restricting the operation of those provisions to disposals for consideration.

11A. Right to information as to terms of disposal, etc.

(1) The requisite majority of qualifying tenants of the constituent flats may serve a notice on the purchaser requiring him—

(a) to give particulars of the terms on which the original disposal was made (including the deposit and consideration required) and the date on which it was made, and

(b) where the disposal consisted of entering into a contract, to provide a copy of the contract.

(2) The notice must specify the name and address of the person to whom (on behalf of the tenants) the particulars are to be given, or the copy of the contract provided.

(3) Any notice under this section must be served before the end of the period of four months beginning with the date by which—

(a) notices under section 3A of the Landlord and Tenant Act 1985 (duty of new landlord to inform tenants of rights) relating to the original disposal, or

(b) where that section does not apply, documents of any other description—

(i) indicating that the original disposal has taken place, and

(ii) alerting the tenants to the existence of their rights under this Part and the time within which any such rights must be exercised,

have been served on the requisite majority or qualifying tenants of the constituent flats.

(4) A person served with a notice under this section shall comply with it within the period of one month beginning with the date on which it is served on him.

12A. Right of qualifying tenants to take benefit of contract

(1) Where the original disposal consisted of entering into a contract, the requisite majority of qualifying tenants of the constituent flats may by notice to the landlord elect that the contract shall have effect as if entered into not with the purchaser but with a person or persons nominated for the purposes of this section by the requisite majority of qualifying tenants of the constituent flats.

(2) Any such notice must be served before the end of the period of six months beginning—

(a) if a notice was served on the purchaser under section 11A (right to information as to terms of disposal, etc.), with the date on which the purchaser complied with that notice;

(b) in any other case, with the date by which documents of any description—

(i) indicating that the original disposal has taken place, and

(ii) alerting the tenants to the existence of their rights under this Part and the time within which any such rights must be exercised,

have been served on the requisite majority of qualifying tenants of the constituent flats.

(3) The notice shall not have effect as mentioned in subsection (1) unless the nominated person—

(a) fulfils any requirements as to the deposit required on entering into the contract, and

(b) fulfils any other conditions required to be fulfilled by the purchaser on entering into the contract.

(4) Unless otherwise agreed, any time limit in the contract as it has effect by virtue of a notice under this section shall start to run again on the service of that notice; and nothing in the contract as it has effect by virtue of a notice under this section shall require the nominated person to complete the purchase before the end of the period of 28 days beginning with the day on which he is deemed to have entered into the contract.

(5) Where the original disposal related to other property in addition to premises to which this Part applied at the time of the disposal—

(a) a notice under this section has effect only in relation to the premises to which this Part applied at the time of the original disposal, and

(b) the terms of the contract shall have effect with any necessary modifications.

In such a case the notice under this section may specify the subject-matter of the disposal, and the terms on which the disposal is to be made (whether doing so expressly or by reference to the original disposal), or may provide for that estate or interest, or any such terms, to be determined by a leasehold valuation tribunal.

12B. Right of qualifying tenants to compel sale, etc. by purchaser

(1) This section applies where—

(a) the original disposal consisted of entering into a contract and no notice has been served under section 12A (right of qualifying tenants to take benefit of contract), or

(b) the original disposal did not consist of entering into a contract.

(2) The requisite majority of qualifying tenants of the constituent flats may serve a notice (a 'purchase notice') on the purchaser requiring him to dispose of the estate or interest that was the subject-matter of the original disposal, on the terms on which it was made (including those relating to

the consideration payable), to a person or persons nominated for the purposes of this section by any such majority of qualifying tenants of those flats.

(3)   Any such notice must be served before the end of the period of six months beginning—

(a)   if a notice was served on the purchaser under section 11A (right to information as to terms of disposal, etc.), with the date on which the purchaser complied with that notice;

(b)   in any other case, with the date by which—

(i)   notices under section 3A of the Landlord and Tenant Act 1985 (duty of new landlord to inform tenants of rights) relating to the original disposal, or

(ii)   where that section does not apply, documents of any other description indicating that the original disposal has taken place, and alerting the tenants to the existence of their rights under this Part and the time within which any such rights must be exercised,

have been served on the requisite majority of qualifying tenants of the constituent flats.

(4)   A purchase notice shall were the original disposal related to other property in addition to premises to which this Part applied at the time of the disposal—

(a)   require the purchaser only to make a disposal relating to those premises, and

(b)   require him to do so on the terms referred to in subsection (2) with any necessary modifications.

In such a case the purchase notice may specify the subject-matter of the disposal, and the terms on which the disposal is to be made (whether doing so expressly or by reference to the original disposal), or may provide for those matters to be determined by a leasehold valuation tribunal.

(5)   Where the property which the purchaser is required to dispose of in pursuance of the purchase notice has since the original disposal become subject to any charge or other incumbrance, then, unless the court by order directs otherwise—

(a)   in the case of a charge to secure the payment of money or the performance of any other obligation by the purchaser or any other person, the instrument by virtue of which the property is disposed of by the purchaser to the person or persons nominated for the purposes of this section shall (subject to the provisions of Part I of Schedule 1) operate to discharge the property from that charge; and

(b)   in the case of any other incumbrance, the property shall be so disposed of subject to the incumbrance but with a reduction in the consideration payable to the purchaser corresponding to the amount by which the existence of the incumbrance reduces the value of the property.

(6)   Subsection (5)(a) and Part I of Schedule 1 apply, with any necessary modifications, to mortgages and liens as they apply to charges; but nothing in those provisions applies to a rentcharge.

(7)   Where the property which the purchaser is required to dispose of in pursuance of the purchase notice has since the original disposal increased in monetary value owing to any change in circumstances (other than a change in the value of money), the amount of the consideration payable to the purchaser for the disposal by him of the property in pursuance of the purchase notice shall be the amount that might reasonably have been obtained on a corresponding disposal made on the open market at the time of the original disposal if the change in circumstances had already taken place.

12C.   Right of qualifying tenants to compel grant of new tenancy by superior landlord

(1)   This section applies where the original disposal consisted of the surrender by the landlord of a tenancy held by him ('the relevant tenancy').

(2)   The requisite majority of qualifying tenants of the constituent flats may serve a notice on the purchaser requiring him to grant a new tenancy of the premises which were subject to the relevant tenancy, on the same terms as those of the relevant tenancy and so as to expire on the same date as that tenancy would have expired, to a person or persons nominated for the purposes of this section by any such majority of qualifying tenants of those flats.

(3)   Any such notice must be served before the end of the period of six months beginning—

(a)   if a notice was served on the purchaser under section 11A (right to information as to terms of disposal, etc.), with the date on which the purchaser complied with that notice;

(b)   in any other case, with the date by which documents of any description—

(i)   indicating that the original disposal has taken place, and

(ii)   alerting the tenants to the existence of their rights under this Part and the time within which any such rights must be exercised,

have been served on the requisite majority of qualifying tenants of the constituent flats.

(4)   If the purchaser paid any amount to the landlord as consideration for the surrender by him of that tenancy, the nominated person shall pay that amount to the purchaser.

(5) Where the premises subject to the relevant tenancy included premises other than premises to which this Part applied at the time of the disposal, a notice under this section shall—

(a) require the purchaser only to grant a new tenancy relating to the premises to which this Part then applied, and

(b) require him to do so on the terms referred to in subsection (2) subject to any necessary modifications.

(6) The purchase notice may specify the subject-matter of the disposal, and the terms on which the disposal is to be made (whether doing so expressly or by reference to the original disposal), or may provide for those matters to be determined by a leasehold valuation tribunal.

12D. Nominated persons: supplementary provisions

(1) The person or persons initially nominated for the purposes of section 12A, 12B or 12C shall be nominated in the notice under that section.

(2) A person nominated for those purposes by the requisite majority of qualifying tenants of the constituent flats may be replaced by another person so nominated if, and only if, he has (for any reason) ceased to be able to act as a nominated person.

(3) Where two or more persons have been nominated and any of them ceases to act without being replaced, the remaining person or persons so nominated may continue to act.

(4) Where, in the exercise of its power to award costs, the court or the Lands Tribunal makes, in connection with any proceedings arising under or by virtue of this Part, an award of costs against the person or persons so nominated, the liability for those costs is a joint and several liability of that person or those persons together with the qualifying tenants by whom the relevant notice was served.

13. Determination of questions by leasehold valuation tribunal

(1) A leasehold valuation tribunal has jurisdiction to hear and determine—

(a) any question arising in relation to any matters specified in a notice under section 12A, 12B or 12C, and

(b) any question arising for determination as mentioned in section 8C(4), 12A(5) or 12B(4) (matters left for determination by tribunal).

(2) On an application under this section the interests of the persons by whom the notice was served under section 12A, 12B or 12C shall be represented by the nominated person; and accordingly the parties to any such application shall not include those persons.

14. Withdrawal of nominated person from transaction under s. 12B or 12C

(1) Where notice has been duly served on the landlord under—

section 12B (right of qualifying tenants to compel sale, etc. by purchaser), or

section 12C (right of qualifying tenants to compel grant of new tenancy by superior landlord),

the nominated person may at any time before a binding contract is entered into in pursuance of the notice, serve notice under this section on the purchaser (a 'notice of withdrawal') indicating an intention no longer to proceed with the disposal.

(2) If at any such time the nominated person becomes aware that the number of qualifying tenants of the constituent flats desiring to proceed with the disposal is less than the requisite majority of those tenants, he shall forthwith serve a notice of withdrawal.

(3) If a notice of withdrawal is served under this section the purchaser may recover from the nominated person any costs reasonably incurred by him in connection with the disposal down to the time when the notice is served on him.

(4) If a notice of withdrawal is served at a time when proceedings arising under or by virtue of this Part are pending before the court or the Lands Tribunal, the liability of the nominated person for any costs incurred by the purchaser as mentioned in subsection (3) shall be such as may be determined by the court or (as the case may be) by the Tribunal.

(5) The costs that may be recovered by the purchaser under this section do not include any costs incurred by him in connection with an application to a leasehold valuation tribunal.

15. Right of qualifying tenants to compel grant of new tenancy by superior landlord

(1) Where—

(a) paragraphs (a) and (b) of section 11(1) apply to a relevant disposal affecting any premises to which at the time of the disposal this Part applied, and

(b) the disposal consisted of the surrender by the landlord of a tenancy held by him ('the relevant tenancy'), and

(c) those premises are still premises to which this Part applies,

the requisite majority of qualifying tenants of the constituent flats may, before the end of the period specified in section 12(2), serve a notice on the new landlord requiring him (except as provided by the following provisions of this Part) to grant a new tenancy of the premises subject to the relevant tenancy, on the terms referred to in subsection (2) below and expiring on the date on which that tenancy would have expired, to a person or persons nominated for the purposes of this section by any such majority of qualifying tenants of those flats.

(2) Those terms are—

(a) the terms of the relevant tenancy; and

(b) if the new landlord paid any amount to the landlord as consideration for the surrender by him of that tenancy, that any such amount is paid to the new landlord by the person or persons so nominated.

(3) A notice under this section—

(a) shall, where the premises subject to the relevant tenancy included premises other than those to which this Part applied at the time of the original disposal—

(i) require the new landlord to grant a new tenancy only of the premises to which this Part so applied, and

(ii) require him to do so on the terms referred to in subsection (2) subject to such modifications as are necessary or expedient in the circumstances;

(b) may, instead of specifying the premises to be demised under the new tenancy or any particular terms on which that tenancy is to be granted by the new landlord (whether doing so expressly or by reference to the relevant tenancy), provide for those premises, or (as the case may be) for any such terms, to be determined by a rent assessment committee in accordance with section 13 (as applied by subsection (4) below).

(4) The following provisions, namely—

section 12(7) to (9)

sections 13 and 14, and

sections 16 and 17,

shall apply in relation to a notice under this section as they apply in relation to a purchase notice (whether referred to as such or as a notice served under section 12(1)) but subject to the modifications specified in subsection (5) below.

(5) Those modifications are as follows—

(a) any reference to the purposes of section 12 shall be read as a reference to the purposes of this section;

(b) the reference in section 13(1)(b) to section 12(3)(b) shall be read as a reference to subsection (3)(b) above;

(c) the references in section 16 to the estate or interest that was the subject-matter of the original disposal shall be read as a reference to the estate or interest which, prior to the surrender of the relevant tenancy, constituted the reversion immediately expectant on it; and

(d)   the references in sections 16 and 17 to sections 12 to 14 shall be read as references to sections 12(7) to (9), 13 and 14 (as applied by subsection (4) above) and this section.

Enforcement by tenants of rights against subsequent purchasers

16.   Rights of qualifying tenants against subsequent purchaser

(1)   This section applies where, at the time when a notice is served on the purchaser under section 11A, 12A, 12B or 12C, he no longer holds the estate or interest that was the subject-matter of the original disposal.

(2)   In the case of a notice under section 11A (right to information as to terms of disposal, etc.) the purchaser shall, within the period for complying with that notice—

(a)   serve notice on the persons specified in the notice as the person to whom particulars are to be provided of the name and address of the person to whom he has disposed of that estate or interest ('the subsequent purchaser'), and

(b)   serve on the subsequent purchaser a copy of the notice under section 11A and of the particulars given by him in response to it.

(3)   In the case of a notice under section 12A, 12B or 12C the purchaser shall forthwith—

(a)   forward the notice to the subsequent purchaser, and

(b)   serve on the nominated person notice of the name and address of the subsequent purchaser.

(4)   Once the purchaser serves a notice in accordance with subsection (2)(a) or (3)(b), sections 12A to 14 shall, instead of applying to the purchaser, apply to the subsequent purchaser as if he were the transferee under the original disposal.

(5)   Subsections (1) to (4) have effect, with any necessary modifications, in a case where, instead of disposing of the whole of the estate or interest referred to in subsection (1) to another person, the purchaser has disposed of it in part or in parts to one or more other persons.

In such a case, sections 12A to 14—

(a)   apply to the purchaser in relation to any part of that estate or interest retained by him, and

(b)   in relation to any part of that estate or interest disposed of to any other person, apply to that other person instead as if he were (as respects that part) the transferee under the original disposal.

Termination of rights against purchasers or subsequent purchasers

17.   Termination of rights against purchaser or subsequent purchaser

(1)   If, at any time after a notice has been served under section 11A, 12A, 12B or 12C, the premises affected by the original disposal cease to be

premises to which this Part applies, the purchaser may serve a notice on the qualifying tenants of the constituent flats stating—

(a) that the premises have ceased to be premises to which this Part applies, and

(b) that any such notice served on him, and anything done in pursuance of it, is to be treated as not having been served or done.

(2) A landlord who has not served such a notice on all of the qualifying tenants of the constituent flats shall nevertheless be treated as having duly served a notice under subsection (1)—

(a) if he has served such a notice on not less than 90% of those tenants, or

(b) where those qualifying tenants number less than ten, if he has served such a notice on all but one of them.

(3) Where a period of three months beginning with the date of service of a notice under section 12A, 12B or 12C on the purchaser has expired—

(a) without any binding contract having been entered into between the purchaser and the nominated person, and

(b) without there having been made any application in connection with the notice to the court or to a leasehold valuation tribunal,

the purchaser may serve on the nominated person a notice stating that the notice, and anything done in pursuance of it, is to be treated as not having been served or done.

(4) Where any such application as is mentioned in subsection (3)(b) was made within the period of three months referred to in that subsection, but—

(a) a period of two months beginning with the date of the determination of that application has expired,

(b) no binding contract has been entered into between the purchaser and the nominated person, and

(c) no other such application as is mentioned in subsequent (3)(b) is pending,

the purchaser may serve on the nominated person a notice stating that any notice served on him under section 12A, 12B or 12C, and anything done in pursuance of any such notice, is to be treated as not having been served or done.

(5) Where the purchaser serves a notice in accordance with subsection (1), (3) or (4), this Part shall cease to have effect in relation to him in connection with the original disposal.

(6) Where a purchaser is entitled to serve a notice under subsection (1) but does not do so, this Part shall continue to have effect in relation to him in connection with the original disposal as if the premises in question were still premises to which this Part applies.

(7)   References in this section to the purchaser include a subsequent purchaser to whom sections 12A to 14 apply by virtue of section 16(4) or (5).

Notices served by prospective purchaser

18.   Notices served by prospective purchasers to ensure that rights of first refusal do not arise
(1)   Where—
(a)   any disposal of an estate or interest in any premises consisting of the whole or part of a building is proposed to be made by a landlord, and
(b)   it appears to the person who would be the transferee under that disposal ('the purchaser') that any such disposal would, or might, be a relevant disposal affecting premises to which this Part applies,
the purchaser may serve notices under this subsection on the tenants of the flats contained in the premises referred to in paragraph (a) ('the flats affected').
(2)   Any notice under subsection (1) shall—
(a)   inform the person on whom it is served of the general nature of the principal terms of the proposed disposal, including in particular—
(i)   the property to which it would relate and the estate or interest in that property proposed to be disposed of by the landlord, and
(ii)   the consideration required by him for making the disposal;
(b)   invite that person to serve a notice on the purchaser stating—
(i)   whether the landlord has served on him, or on any predecessor in title of his, a notice under section 5 with respect to the disposal, and
(ii)   if the landlord has not so served any such notice, whether he is aware of any reason why he is not entitled to be served with any such notice by the landlord, and
(iii)   if he is not so aware, whether he would wish to avail himself of the right of first refusal conferred by any such notice if it were served; and
(c)   inform that person of the effect of the following provisions of this section.
(3)   Where the purchaser has served notices under subsection (1) on at least 80 per cent of the tenants of the flats affected and—
(a)   not more than 50 per cent of the tenants on whom those notices have been served by the purchaser have served notices on him in pursuance of subsection (2)(b) by the end of the period of 28 days beginning with the date on which the last of them was served by him with a notice under this section, or

    (b)   more than 50 per cent of the tenants on whom those notices have been served by the purchaser have served notices on him in pursuance of subsection (2)(b) but the notices in each case indicate that the tenant serving it either—

        (i)   does not regard himself as being entitled to be served by the landlord with a notice under section 5 with respect to the disposal, or

        (ii)   would not wish to avail himself of the right of first refusal conferred by such a notice if it were served,

the premises affected by the disposal shall, in relation to the disposal, be treated for the purposes of this Part as premises to which this Part does not apply.

    (4)   For the purposes of subsection (3) each of the flats affected shall be regarded as having one tenant, who shall count towards any of the percentages specified in that subsection whether he is a qualifying tenant of the flat or not.

Supplementary

18A.   The requisite majority of qualifying tenants

    (1)   In this Part 'the requisite majority of qualifying tenants of the constituent flats' means qualifying tenants of constituent flats with more than 50 per cent of the available votes.

    (2)   The total number of available votes shall be determined as follows—

    (a)   where an offer notice has been served under section 5, that number is equal to the total number of constituent flats let to qualifying tenants on the date when the period specified in that notice as the period for accepting the offer expires;

    (b)   where a notice is served under section 11A without a notice having been previously served under section 5, that number is equal to the total number of constituent flats let to qualifying tenants on the date of service of the notice under section 11A;

    (c)   where a notice is served under section 12A, 12B or 12C without a notice having been previously served under section 5 or section 11A, that number is equal to the total number of constituent flats let to qualifying tenants on the date of service of the notice under section 12A, 12B or 12C, as the case may be.

    (3)   There is one available vote in respect of each of the flats so let on the date referred to in the relevant paragraph of subsection (2), which shall be attributed to the qualifying tenant to whom it is let.

    (4)   The persons constituting the requisite majority of qualifying tenants for one purpose may be different from the persons constituting such a majority for another purpose.

19. Enforcement of obligations under Part I

(1)   The court may, on the application of any person interested, make an order requiring any person who has made default in complying with any duty imposed on him by any provision of this Part to make good the default within such time as is specified in the order.

(2)   An application shall not be made under subsection (1) unless—

(a)   a notice has been previously served on the person in question requiring him to make good the default, and

(b)   more than 14 days have elapsed since the date of service of that notice without his having done so.

(3)   The restriction imposed by section 1(1) may be enforced by an injunction granted by the court.

20. Construction of Part I and power of Secretary of State to prescribe modifications

(1)   In this Part—

'acceptance notice' has the meaning given by section 6(3);

'associated company', in relation to a body corporate, means another body corporate which is (within the meaning of section 736 of the Companies Act 1985) that body's holding company, a subsidiary of that body or another subsidiary of that body's holding company;

'constituent flat' shall be construed in accordance with section 5(1) or 11(2), as the case may require;

'disposal' shall be construed in accordance with section 4(3) and section 4A (application of provisions to contracts), and references to the acquisition of an estate or interest shall be construed accordingly;

'landlord', in relation to any premises, shall be construed in accordance with section 2;

'the nominated person' means the person or persons for the time being nominated by the requisite majority of the qualifying tenants of the constituent flats for the purposes of section 6, 12A, 12B or 12C, as the case may require;

'offer notice' means a notice served by a landlord under section 5;

'the original disposal' means the relevant disposal referred to in section 11(1);

'the protected interest' means the estate, interest or other subject-matter of an offer notice;

'the protected period' has the meaning given by section 6(4);

'purchase notice' has the meaning given by section 12B(2);

'purchaser' has the meaning given by section 11(3);

'qualifying tenant', in relation to a flat, shall be construed in accordance with section 3;

'relevant disposal' shall be construed in accordance with section 4;

'the requisite majority', in relation to qualifying tenants, shall be construed in accordance with section 18A;

'transferee', in relation to a disposal, shall be construed in accordance with section 4(3).

(2)   In this Part—

(a)   any reference to an offer is a reference to an offer made subject to contract, and

(b)   any reference to the acceptance of an offer is a reference to its acceptance subject to contract.

(3)   Any reference in this Part to a tenant of a particular description shall be construed, in relation to any time when the interest under his tenancy has ceased to be vested in him, as a reference to the person who is for the time being the successor in title to that interest.

(4)   The Secretary of State may by regulations make such modifications of any of the provisions of sections 5 to 18 as he considers appropriate, and any such regulations may contain such incidental, supplemental or transitional provisions as he considers appropriate in connection with the regulations.

(5)   In subsection (4) 'modifications' includes additions, omissions and alterations.

. . .

58.   Exempt landlords and resident landlords

(1)   In this Act 'exempt landlord' means a landlord who is one of the following bodies, namely—

(a)   a district, county or London borough council, the Common Council of the City of London, the Council of the Isles of Scilly, the Inner London Education Authority, or a joint authority established by Part IV of the Local Government Act 1985;

(b)   the Commission for the New Towns or a development corporation established by an order made (or having effect as if made) under the New Towns Act 1981;

(c)   an urban development corporation within the meaning of Part XVI of the Local Government, Planning and Land Act 1980;

(ca)   a housing action trust established under Part III of the Housing Act 1988.

(d)   the Development Board for Rural Wales;

(e)   the Housing Corporation;

(f)   a housing trust (as defined in section 6 of the Housing Act 1985) which is a charity;

(g)   a registered housing association, or an unregistered housing association which is a fully mutual housing association, within the meaning of the Housing Associations Act 1985; or

(h)   an authority established under section 10 of the Local Government Act 1985 (joint arrangements for waste disposal functions).

(2)   For the purposes of this Act the landlord of any premises consisting of the whole or part of a building is a resident landlord of those premises at any time if—

(a)   the premises are not, and do not form part of, a purpose-built block of flats; and

(b)   at that time the landlord occupies a flat contained in the premises as his only or principal residence; and

(c)   he has so occupied such a flat throughout a period of not less than 12 months ending with that time.

(3)   In subsection (2) 'purpose-built block of flats' means a building which contained as constructed, and contains, two or more flats.

59.   Meaning of 'lease', 'long lease' and related expressions

(1)   In this Act 'lease' and 'tenancy' have the same meaning; and both expressions include—

(a)   a sub-lease or sub-tenancy, and

(b)   an agreement for a lease or tenancy (or for a sub-lease or sub-tenancy).

(2)   The expressions 'landlord' and 'tenant', and references to letting, to the grant of a lease or to covenants or the terms of a lease shall be construed accordingly.

(3)   In this Act 'long lease' means—

(a)   a lease granted for a term certain exceeding 21 years, whether or not it is (or may become) terminable before the end of that term by notice given by the tenant or by re-entry of forfeiture;

(b)   a lease for a term fixed by law under a grant with a covenant or obligation for perpetual renewal, other than a lease by sub-demise from one which is not a long lease; or

(c)   a lease granted in pursuance of Part V of the Housing Act 1985 (the right to buy).

60.   General interpretation

(1)   In this Act—

'the 1985 Act' means the Landlord and Tenant Act 1985;

'charity' means a charity within the meaning of the Charities Act 1993, and 'charitable purposes', in relation to a charity, means charitable purposes whether of that charity or of that charity and other charities;

'common parts', in relation to any building or part of a building, includes the structure and exterior of that building or part and any common facilities within it;

'the court' means the High Court or a county court;

'dwelling' means a building or part of a building occupied or intended to be occupied as a separate dwelling, together with any yard, garden, outhouses and appurtenances belonging to it or usually enjoyed with it;

'exempt landlord' has the meaning given by section 58(1);

'flat' means a separate set of premises, whether or not on the same floor, which—

(a) forms part of a building, and

(b) is divided horizontally from some other part of that building, and

(c) is constructed or adapted for use for the purposes of a dwelling;

'functional land', in relation to a charity, means land occupied by the charity, or by trustees for it, and wholly or mainly used for charitable purposes;

'landlord' (except for the purposes of Part I) means the immediate landlord or, in relation to a statutory tenant, the person who, apart from the statutory tenancy, would be entitled to possession of the premises subject to the tenancy;

'lease' and related expressions shall be construed in accordance with section 59(1) and (2);

'long lease' has the meaning given by section 59(3);

'mortgage' includes any charge or lien, and references to a mortgagee shall be construed accordingly;

'notices in proceedings' means notices or other documents served in, or in connection with, any legal proceedings;

'resident landlord' shall be construed in accordance with section 58(2);

'statutory tenancy' and 'statutory tenant' mean a statutory tenancy or statutory tenant within the meaning of the Rent Act 1977 or the Rent (Agriculture) Act 1976;

'tenancy' includes a statutory tenancy.

SCHEDULES

Sections 12 and 32   SCHEDULE 1
DISCHARGE OF MORTGAGES ETC.: SUPPLEMENTARY PROVISIONS

PART I

DISCHARGE IN PURSUANCE OF PURCHASE NOTICES

Construction

1. In this Part of this Schedule—
'the consideration payable' means the consideration payable to the purchaser for the disposal by him of the property referred to in section 12B(7);
'the purchaser' has the same meaning as in section 12, and accordingly includes any person to whom that section applies by virtue of section 16(4) or (5); and
'the nominated person' means the person or persons nominated as mentioned in section 12B(2).

Duty of nominated person to redeem mortgages

2.—(1) Where in accordance with section 12B(5)(a) an instrument will operate to discharge any property from a charge to secure the payment of money, it shall be the duty of the nominated person to apply the consideration payable, in the first instance, in or towards the redemption of any such charge (and, if there are more than one, then according to their priorities).

(2) Where sub-paragraph (1) applies to any charge or charges, then if (and only if) the consideration payable is applied by the nominated person in accordance with that sub-paragraph or paid into court by him in accordance with paragraph 4, the instrument in question shall operate as mentioned in sub-paragraph (1) notwithstanding that the consideration payable is insufficient to enable the charge or charges to be redeemed in its or their entirety.

(3) Subject to sub-paragraph (4), sub-paragraph (1) shall not apply to a charge which is a debenture holders' charge, that is to say, a charge (whether a floating charge or not) in favour of the holders of a series of debentures issued by a company or other body of persons, or in favour of trustees for such debenture holders; and any such charge shall be disregarded in determining priorities for the purposes of sub-paragraph (1).

(4) Sub-paragraph (3) above shall not have effect in relation to a charge in favour of trustees for debenture holders which at the date of the instrument by virtue of which the property is disposed of by the purchaser is (as regards that property) a specific and not a floating charge.

Determination of amounts due in respect of mortgages

3.—(1) For the purpose of determining the amount payable in respect of any charge under paragraph 2(1), a person entitled to the benefit of a charge to which that provision applies shall not be permitted to exercise any right to consolidate that charge with a separate charge on other property.

(2) For the purpose of discharging any property from a charge to which paragraph 2(1) applies, a person may be required to accept three months or any longer notice of the intention to pay the whole or part of the principal secured by the charge, together with interest to the date of payment, notwithstanding that the terms of the security make other provision or no provision as to the time and manner of payment; but he shall be entitled, if he so requires, to receive such additional payment as is reasonable in the circumstances in respect of the costs of re-investment or other incidental costs and expenses and in respect of any reduction in the rate of interest obtainable on re-investment.

Payments into court

4.—(1) Where under section 12B(5)(a) any property is to be discharged from a charge and, in accordance with paragraph 2(1), a person is or may be entitled in respect of the charge to receive the whole or part of the consideration payable, then if—

(a) for any reason difficulty arises in ascertaining how much is payable in respect of the charge, or

(b) for any reason mentioned in sub-paragraph (2) below difficulty arises in making a payment in respect of the charge,
the nominated person may pay into court on account of the consideration payable the amount, if known, of the payment to be made in respect of the charge or, if that amount is not known, the whole of that consideration or such lesser amount as the nominated person thinks right in order to provide for that payment.

(2) Payment may be made into court in accordance with sub-paragraph (1)(b) where the difficulty arises for any of the following reasons, namely—

(a) because a person who is or may be entitled to receive payment cannot be found or ascertained;

(b) because any such person refuses or fails to make out a title, or to accept payment and give a proper discharge, or to take any steps reasonably required of him to enable the sum payable to be ascertained and paid; or

(c) because a tender of the sum payable cannot, by reason of complications in the title to it or the want of two or more trustees or for other reasons, be effected, or not without incurring or involving unreasonable cost or delay.

(3)   Without prejudice to sub-paragraph (1)(a), the whole or part of the consideration payable shall be paid into court by the nominated person if, before execution of the instrument referred to in paragraph 2(1), notice is given to him—

(a)   that the purchaser or a person entitled to the benefit of a charge on the property in question requires him to do so for the purpose of protecting the rights of persons so entitled, or for reasons related to the bankruptcy or winding up of the purchaser, or

(b)   that steps have been taken to enforce any charge on the purchaser's interest in that property by the bringing of proceedings in any court, or by the appointment of a receiver or otherwise;

and where payment into court is to be made by reason only of a notice under this sub-paragraph, and the notice is given with reference to proceedings in a court specified in the notice other than a county court, payment shall be made into the court so specified.

Savings

5.—(1)   Where any property is discharged by section 12B(5)(a) from a charge (without the obligations secured by the charge being satisfied by the receipt of the whole or part of the consideration payable), the discharge of that property from the charge shall not prejudice any right or remedy for the enforcement of those obligations against other property comprised in the same or any other security, nor prejudice any personal liability as principal or otherwise of the purchaser or any other person.

(2)   Nothing in this Schedule shall be construed as preventing a person from joining in the instrument referred to in paragraph 2(1) for the purpose of discharging the property in question from any charge without payment or for a lesser payment than that to which he would otherwise be entitled; and, if he does so, the persons to whom the consideration payable ought to be paid shall be determined accordingly.

PART II
DISCHARGE IN PURSUANCE OF ACQUISITION ORDERS

Construction

6.   In this Part of this Schedule—
'the consideration payable' means the consideration payable for the acquisition of the landlord's interest referred to in section 32(1); and 'the nominated person' means the person or persons nominated for the purposes of Part III by the persons who applied for the acquisition order in question.

Duty of nominated person to redeem mortgages

7.—(1)   Where in accordance with section 32(1) an instrument will operate to discharge any premises from a charge to secure the payment of money, it shall be the duty of the nominated person to apply the consideration payable, in the first instance, in or towards the redemption of any such charge (and, if there are more than one, then according to their priorities).

(2)   Where sub-paragraph (1) applies to any charge or charges, then if (and only if) the consideration payable is applied by the nominated person in accordance with that sub-paragraph or paid into court by him in accordance with paragraph 9, the instrument in question shall operate as mentioned in sub-paragraph (1) notwithstanding that the consideration payable is insufficient to enable the charge or charges to be redeemed in its or their entirety.

(3)   Subject to sub-paragraph (4), sub-paragraph (1) shall not apply to a charge which is a debenture holders' charge within the meaning of paragraph 2(3) in Part I of this Schedule; and any such charge shall be disregarded in determining priorities for the purposes of sub-paragraph (1).

(4)   Sub-paragraph (3) above shall not have effect in relation to a charge in favour of trustees for debenture holders which at the date of the instrument by virtue of which the landlord's interest in the premises in question is acquired is (as regards those premises) a specific and not a floating charge.

Determination of amounts due in respect of mortgages

8.—(1)   For the purpose of determining the amount payable in respect of any charge under paragraph 7(1), a person entitled to the benefit of a charge to which that provision applies shall not be permitted to exercise any right to consolidate that charge with a separate charge on other property.

(2)   For the purpose of discharging any premises from a charge to which paragraph 7(1) applies, a person may be required to accept three months or any longer notice of the intention to pay the whole or part of the principal secured by the charge, together with interest to the date of payment, notwithstanding that the terms of the security make other provision or no provision as to the time and manner of payment; but he shall be entitled, if he so requires, to receive such additional payment as is reasonable in the circumstances in respect of the costs of re-investment or other incidental costs and expenses and in respect of any reduction in the rate of interest obtainable on re-investment.

Payments into court

9.—(1)   Where under section 32 any premises are to be discharged from a charge and, in accordance with paragraph 7(1), a person is or may be entitled in respect of the charge to receive the whole or part of the consideration payable, then if—

(a)   for any reason difficulty arises in ascertaining how much is payable in respect of the charge, or

(b)   for any reason mentioned in sub-paragraph (2) below difficulty arises in making a payment in respect of the charge,

the nominated person may pay into court on account of the consideration payable the amount, if known, of the payment to be made in respect of the charge or, if that amount is not known, the whole of that consideration or such lesser amount as the nominated person thinks right in order to provide for that payment.

(2)   Payment may be made into court in accordance with sub-paragraph (1)(b) where the difficulty arises for any of the following reasons, namely—

(a)   because a person who is or may be entitled to receive payment cannot be found or ascertained;

(b)   because any such person refuses or fails to make out a title, or to accept payment and give a proper discharge, or to take any steps reasonably required of him to enable the sum payable to be ascertained and paid; or

(c)   because a tender of the sum payable cannot, by reason of complications in the title to it or the want of two or more trustees or for other reasons, be effected, or not without incurring or involving unreasonable cost or delay.

(3)   Without prejudice to sub-paragraph (1)(a), the whole or part of the consideration payable shall be paid into court by the nominated person if, before execution of the instrument referred to in paragraph 7(1), notice is given to him—

(a)   that the landlord or a person entitled to the benefit of a charge on the premises in question requires him to do so for the purpose of protecting the rights of persons so entitled, or for reasons related to the bankruptcy or winding up of the landlord, or

(b)   that steps have been taken to enforce any charge on the landlord's interest in those premises by the bringing of proceedings in any court, or by the appointment of a receiver or otherwise;

and where payment into court is to be made by reason only of a notice under this sub-paragraph, and the notice is given with reference to proceedings in a court specified in the notice other than a county court, payment shall be made into the court so specified.

Savings

10.—(1) Where any premises are discharged by section 32 from a charge (without the obligations secured by the charge being satisfied by the receipt of the whole or part of the consideration payable), the discharge of those premises from the charge shall not prejudice any right or remedy for the enforcement of those obligations against other property comprised in the same or any other security, nor prejudice any personal liability as principal or otherwise of the landlord or any other person.

(2) Nothing in this Schedule shall be construed as preventing a person from joining in the instrument referred to in paragraph 7(1) for the purpose of discharging the premises in question from any charge without payment or for a lesser payment than that to which he would otherwise be entitled; and, if he does so, the persons to whom the consideration payable ought to be paid shall be determined accordingly.

Forms for Use under the Landlord and Tenant Act 1987, Part I

FORM 1

NOTICE PURSUANT TO THE PROVISIONS OF THE LANDLORD AND TENANT ACT 1987 (AS AMENDED BY THE HOUSING ACT 1996) ('the Act')

Notice:	Section 5A Notice by the Landlord to the Tenants in case of sale by contract to be completed by conveyance
Property:	
Tenure:	
Headlease:	
Landlord:	
Landlord's Solicitors:	
Title Number:	
Consideration:	£
Deposit:	£
Principal Terms of Contract:	To be sold subject to the Standard Conditions of Sale (Third Edition) and subject as set out below:—

1. The Landlord's interest is registered at HM Land Registry with the Title Number

2. The Property is sold with [Full/Limited] Title Guarantee and subject to all matters referred to in the registers of the Title Number other than charges to secure money.
3. Completion shall take place on or before a date 28 days after exchange of contracts pursuant to this notice.
4. [On completion of any transfer of the Property the Buyer shall pay to the Landlord the amount of arrears of ground rent, service charge or other sums lawfully due to the Landlord in addition to the consideration.]

TAKE NOTICE THAT:

1. The Landlord proposes to dispose of its interest in the Property pursuant to contract. This notices constitutes an offer by the Landlord to enter into a contract on the above principal terms which may be accepted by the requisite majority of qualifying tenants of the flats in the Property.
2. This offer may be accepted within a period of two months and one day from the date of service of this notice. Unless you are given further notice to the contrary this notice will have been deemed to have been served within two days after posting by first class post to you or on the day after delivery if this notice has been delivered by hand.
3. On or before a date two months and one day after the expiry of the date specified in paragraph 2 above you must nominate a person for the purpose of Section 6 of the Act into whose name the Property is to be transferred.

ANY NOTICE TO BE SERVED ON THE LANDLORD IS TO BE SERVED UPON THE LANDLORD'S SOLICITORS

Signed ....
(As agent for the Landlord)
Dated ....

Notes

1. Section 3 of the Act: definition of a qualifying tenant.
2. Section 2 of the Act: definition of a landlord.
3. Section 18A of the Act: definition of the requisite majority which is more than 50 per cent of the available votes.
4. Section 5(1) and (3) of the Act: definition of the constituent flats which are the flats in the building.

FORM 2

NOTICE PURSUANT TO THE PROVISIONS
OF THE LANDLORD AND TENANT ACT 1987
(AS AMENDED BY THE HOUSING ACT 1996) ('the Act')

Notice: Section 5A Notice by the Landlord to the Tenants in case of sale by contract to be completed by conveyance

Property:
Tenure:
Landlord:
Landlord's Solicitors:
Title Number:
Principal Terms of Contract: To be sold subject to the Standard Conditions of Sale (Third Edition) and on the terms of the Agreement annexed hereto

TAKE NOTICE THAT:

1. The Landlord proposes to dispose of its interest in the Property pursuant to contract. This notice constitutes an offer by the Landlord to enter into a contract on the above terms which may be accepted by the requisite majority of qualifying tenants of the flats in the Property.
2. This offer may be accepted within a period of two months and one day from the date of service of this notice. Unless you are given further notice to the contrary this notice will have been deemed to be served within two days after posting by first class post to you or the day after delivery if this notice has been delivered by hand.
3. On or before a date two months and one day after the expiry of the date specified in paragraph 2 above you must nominate a person for the purpose of Section 6 of the Act into whose name the Property is to be transferred.

ANY NOTICE TO BE SERVED ON THE LANDLORD IS TO BE SERVED UPON THE LANDLORD'S SOLICITORS

Signed ....
(As agent for the Landlord)
Dated ....

Notes

1. Section 3 of the Act: Definition of a qualifying tenant.
2. Section 2 of the Act: Definition of a landlord.
3. Section 18A of the Act: Definition of the requisite majority which is more than 50 per cent of the available votes.
4. Section 5(1) and (3) of the Act: Definition of the constituent flats which are the flats in the building.

<u>AGREEMENT: DATED</u>   **1998**

1. PARTICULARS

1.1 Seller

1.2 Buyer

1.3 Property

1.4 Title Number

1.5 [Headlease]

1.6 Title Guarantee   [Full/Limited]

1.7 Completion Date

1.8 Purchase Price   £

1.9 Deposit   £

1.10 Buyer's Solicitors

2. DEFINITIONS AND INTERPRETATIONS

Unless the context otherwise requires, the expressions defined in clauses 1 and 2 hereof shall have the meanings specified in this Agreement:—

2.1 'the Agreement' means this Agreement

2.2 'the Completion Date' means the date of completion of the sale and purchase of the Property hereunder which will be a date on or before twenty-eight days from the date hereof

2.3 'the Draft Transfer' means a Transfer in the form of the draft annexed hereto marked 'Draft Transfer'

2.4 'the Interest Rate' means three per centum above the base lending rate of Lloyds Bank plc

2.5 'the Property' means the land and Property which is more fully described in the Draft Transfer and comprised in the Title Number

2.6 'the Seller's Solicitors' means

2.7   'the Seller's Solicitors' Bank Account' means

2.8   'the Standard Conditions of Sale' means the Standard Conditions of Sale (Third Edition)

2.9   words importing the masculine gender include the feminine and the neuter and vice versa

2.10   words importing the singular include the plural and vice versa

2.11   references to persons include bodies corporate and vice versa

2.12   save where the context otherwise requires all obligations given or undertaken by more than one person in the same capacity are given or undertaken by them jointly and severally

2.13   the clause headings shall not affect the construction of the Agreement

2.14   save as indicated to the contrary any reference to a numbered clause means the clause in the Agreement which is so numbered

3. AGREEMENT FOR SALE

The Seller shall sell and the Buyer shall purchase the Property at the Purchase Price in accordance with the terms of the Agreement.

4. PURCHASE PRICE DEPOSIT AND COMPLETION

4.1   The Purchaser shall on the execution of the Agreement pay the Deposit to the Seller's Solicitors as agent and condition 2.2 of the Standard Conditions of Sale shall be read accordingly.

4.2   On the Completion Date the Buyers shall pay to the Seller's Solicitors the Purchase Price less the Deposit.

4.3   Completion of the sale and purchase of the Property hereunder and payment of the balance of the Purchase Price referred to in Clause 4.2 hereof together with interest on any unpaid sums due and payable under the terms of the Agreement at the Interest Rate (to be calculated from the date hereof) shall take place at the offices of the Seller's Solicitors and in the event of the Seller's Solicitors agreeing to receive the said sum by means of bank telegraphic transfer such monies shall be deemed to be received (for the purposes of the Standard Conditions of Sale) when they are credited to the Seller's Solicitors' Bank Account.

4.4   If the Buyer shall fail to complete on the Completion Date the Buyer shall be and become liable to pay and indemnify the Seller for its legal costs of and incidental to the preparation and service of a notice to complete and all additional work consequent upon the Buyer's default such costs being not less than One Hundred and Fifty Pounds plus VAT payable and the Seller shall be entitled to retain the title deeds until such sum and any interest payable has been paid.

4.5 In the event of the Buyer failing to complete on the Completion Date the Seller will be entitled to charge [both rent under the terms of the tenancies and] interest under the terms of the contract up to and including the date of actual completion.

5. TITLE

5.1 The Seller's title to the Property is registered at HM Land Registry under the Title Number and the Seller sells with the Title Guarantee.

5.2 The Property is [Freehold/Leasehold] Property.

6. TRANSFER

The assurance to the Property shall be in the form of the Draft [Transfer/Lease] which shall be prepared in duplicate by the Seller's Solicitors and executed by the Buyers and delivered to the Seller's Solicitors on or before the Completion Date.

7. INCUMBRANCES

The Property is sold subject to and (where appropriate) with the benefit of:—

7.1 The agreements declarations exceptions and reservations rights and privileges covenants and conditions and all other matters contained or referred to in the registers of the Title Number and the Seller having deduced to the Buyer title to the Property the Buyer accepts such title and no objection or requisition shall be made by or on behalf of the Buyer to any matter concerning or arising out of such title.

7.2 The tenancies (if any) relating thereto and the Buyer or his Solicitor have been afforded the opportunity or inspecting the Tenancies or copies and all other deeds and documents relating to the property in the Seller's possession as the Buyer hereby admits the Buyer shall (whether or not he has so inspected) be deemed to purchase the Property with full knowledge of the contents thereof and shall raise no objection or requisition thereto.

7.3 The rights (if any) of any person under any tenancy or other occupation or right derived out of the Property.

8. RENTS AND SERVICE CHARGES

8.1 This clause shall apply in respect of any lease or tenancy (a 'tenancy') which at the date hereof or the date of actual completion affects the Property.

8.2 If on the date of actual completion there are any arrears of rent insurance premiums service charge payments or other sums lawfully then due to the Seller under the terms of a Tenancy then the Buyer shall pay such arrears to the Seller on completion and on completion the Seller will if required by the Buyer execute a deed of assignment of such arrears to the Buyer in a form to be agreed between the Seller and the Buyer.

8.3 If following completion the Seller shall receive any rent service charges or other payments made pursuant to any Tenancy the Seller shall account to Buyer for such monies within a reasonable period of receipt of the same.

8.4 The provision of this sub-clause shall apply if in respect of any Tenancy there are monies held by or on behalf of the Seller in respect or on account of any service charge or contribution towards the costs of supplying service or undertaking works or other matters for the benefit of the whole or part of the Property (a 'Service Charge Fund').

8.5 The Seller may on completion deduct from the Service Charge Fund an amount in respect of expenditure actually incurred by the Seller having produced first receipts of such expenditure to the Buyer in connection with its obligations under any Tenancy but on completion shall pay over to the Buyer the balance (if any) of the Service Charge Fund less the amount of any tax payable by the Seller in connection with the same.

8.6 Insofar as any such expenditure shall exceed the balance held in the relevant Service Charge Fund such expenditure shall be reimbursed to the Seller by the Buyer on completion.

8.7 The Buyer will on completion assume responsibility for all Landlord's electricity and other utility supplies in respect of the Property.

8.8 The Seller shall on completion pay by way of deduction from the Purchase Price the amount of all rental bonds in respect of all Tenancies currently held by the Seller to the Buyer.

9. HEADLEASE

9.1 In respect of the Headlease taken subject to payment of ground rent service charge insurance premium or any other sums properly payable by the Seller the Seller shall be responsible for any such sums which relate to a period prior to the Completion Date provided that demands for such sums are received be the Seller prior to the Completion Date provided that demands for such sums are received by the Seller prior to the Completion Date but it is hereby agreed (subject to paragraph 2 of this condition) that the Seller shall not be responsible for any sums for which demands are received after the Completion Date whether or not they relate to a period prior to the Completion Date.

9.2 Where interim service charge payments are paid on account under the terms of the Headlease and final accounts are made up after the end of an accounting period and it is anticipated that there shall be a deficit or a surplus in the account giving rise to a liability for excess service charge or an entitlement to a credit on the account (as the case may be) then an apportionment shall be made at completion and in the absence of any accounts according to the best estimate of the Seller whose decision shall be final.

9.3 Any apportionment made under paragraphs 1 and 2 of this condition shall be final and binding upon the parties (and if no apportionment is made it shall be deemed to be an apportionment for the purposes of this condition) and the Buyer shall indemnify the Seller in respect of all proceedings actions claims demands and other liability (whether arising before or after completion) for the sums referred to in this condition and all other obligations whatsoever arising in respect of or in connection with the Property.

9.4 All apportionments pursuant to this clause are to be made with effect from the Completion Date.

9.5 Any sums paid in advance in respect of future work not commenced by the Completion Date or which are held in a general sinking fund shall be reimbursed to the Seller on completion and any sums to be paid after the Completion Date shall be the responsibility of the Buyer.

9.6 No express or implied covenant is given by the Seller to the Buyer that there is no subsisting breach of any condition or tenant's obligations contained within the Headlease.

10. DOCUMENTATION

The Buyer will not raise any requisition or objection in relation to the absence of any Lease Tenancy Agreement or other documentation relating to any part of the Property and will be deemed to purchase subject to all terms of any such agreement which the Seller is unable to produce.

11. OTHER MATTERS AFFECTING THE PROPERTY

The Property is also sold subject to:—

11.1 All local land charges whether registered or not before the date hereof and all matters capable of registration as local land charges whether or not so registered.

11.2 All notices served and orders demands proposals or requirements or other matters made by any local public or other competent authority whether before or after the date hereof.

11.3 All actual or proposed charges notices orders restrictions agreements conditions contraventions or other matters arising under the Town and Country Planning Act 1990.

11.4 All easements quasi-easements rights (whether public or private) light support drainage water and electricity supplies and other exceptions or other similar matters whether or not apparent on inspection or disclosed in any of the documents referred to herein.

11.5 All (if any) such matters as a re referred to in Section 70 Land Registration Act 1925 and the Buyer hereby indemnifies the Seller against any liability of the Seller arising out of any of the above.

12. DISCLAIMER

The Buyer admits:—

12.1 That they have inspected the property and purchase the same with full knowledge and notice of the state and condition of the same in all respects and of the easements rights and privileges (if any) affecting the same.

12.2 That they enter into the Agreement solely as a result of their own inspection and on the basis of the replies of the relevant authorities to enquiries and the terms of this Clause 14 and not upon any representation or warranty either written oral or implied or whether contained in any advertisement particulars or other matters made by or on behalf of the Seller (save for any such contained in written replies given by the Seller's Solicitors to any preliminary equiries raised by the Buyers' Solicitors prior to the date hereof).

12.3 That notwithstanding the foregoing provisions the Seller does not hereby or in any other way give or make nor has given or made at any other time any representation or warranty that any use of the Property or the activities carried thereon is or will be or will remain a permitted use or activity within the provisions of the Town and Country Planning Act 1990 or any legislation orders or directions amending the same or supplemental thereto and the Buyer shall raise no further enquiry requisition or objection in this regard.

12.4 That the Agreement contains the entire agreement between the parties.

13. NON-ASSIGNMENT

The Buyer shall not assign or part in any way with the benefit of the Agreement or any part thereof nor shall the Seller be required to convey or transfer the Property to any person other than the Buyer nor in more than one lot nor at a price apportioned between different parts of the Property.

14. INSURANCE

The Seller shall (if it already does so) procure the maintenance of the insurance of the Properties until completion save insofar as such insurance is the responsibility of any lessee and on completion the Seller shall procure the cancellation of its insurance insofar as it affects the Property and any premium refund relating to the period after the date of actual completion shall if the premium has been paid or reimbursed by any lessee or tenant to the Seller be accounted for by the Seller to the Buyer but if the premium has not been paid or reimbursed by the lessee or tenant shall be retained by the Seller.

15. INDEMNITY

The Buyer confirms that it will be responsible for and keep the Seller fully and effectually indemnified against all damage damages losses costs expenses actions demands proceedings claims and liabilities made against or suffered or incurred by the Seller arising directly or indirectly out of any claim under any tenancy.

16. MANAGEMENT

The Seller shall be entitled to continue to manage the Property up to actual completion (either by itself or through any managing agent) and in particular may:—

16.1 Perform its covenants or obligations under any tenancy.

16.2 Grant or withhold licences consents approvals and deeds of variation and rectification on such terms as it deems appropriate.

16.3 Issue or defend proceedings.

17. **STANDARD CONDITIONS OF SALE**

Subject as hereinbefore mentioned the Standard Conditions of Sale shall apply to the Agreement in so far as they are applicable to a sale by private treaty and are not inconsistent with the terms of the Agreement but subject to:

17.1 The exclusion from this Agreement of the following conditions
4.1
4.2
4.3.2
4.5
5.1.1 and 5.1.2

17.1 The deletion of the word 'and' and the substitution of the word 'or' therefor in condition 1.1.1(c).

17.2 The deletion of the words '2.00pm' and the substitution of the words '12.00 noon' therefor in conditions 6.1.2 and 6.1.3.

17.3 The addition of the words 'or (at the discretion of the Vendor) enforce payment of the deposit as a deposit by suing on the cheque or otherwise' to condition 2.2.4.

18. **NON-MERGER**

The provisions of the Agreement shall not merge on completion so far as they remain to be performed and are capable of taking effect thereafter and shall remain in full force and effect notwithstanding completion of the sale and purchase of the Property hereunder.

AS WITNESS the hands of the parties hereto the day and year first before written

SELLER

BUYER

Transfer of whole
of registered title (s)

H M Land Registry

Stamp Duty

Place "X" in the box that applies and complete the box in the appropriate certificate

☐ I/We hereby certify that this instrument falls within category   ☐ in the Schedule to the Stamp Duty (Exempt
Instruments) Regulations 1987

☐ It is certified that the transaction effected does not form part of a larger transaction or of a series of transactions in
Respect of which the amount or value or the aggregate amount or value of the consideration exceeds the sum of

☐

---

1. Title Number(s) of the Property

2. Property

   If this transfer is made under section 37 of the Land Registration Act 1925 following a not-yet-registered dealing with part only of the land in a title, or is made under rule 72 of the Land Registration Rules 1925, include a reference to the last preceding document of title containing a description of the property.

3. Date   1998

4. Transferor

5. Transferee **for entry on the register**

6. Transferee's intended **address(es) for service in the U.K.** *(including postcode)* **for entry on the register**

7. **The Transferor transfers the property to the Transferee**

8. Consideration *(Place "X" in the box that applies)*

   ☐ The Transferor has received from the Transferee for the property the sum of £360000.00 (Three hundred and sixty thousand pounds)

   ☐ The Transfer is not for money or anything which has a monetary value

9. The Transferor transfers with *(place "X" in the box which applies and add any modifications)*

   ☐ full title guarantee   ☐ limited title guarantee

10. Declaration of trust *Where there is more than one transferee, place "X" in the appropriate box*

☐ The transferees are to hold the property on trust for themselves as joint tenants

☐ The transferees are to hold the property on trust for themselves as tenants in common in equal shares

☐ The transferees are to hold the property *(complete as necessary)*

11. Additional Provision(s)

The Transferee with the object of affording to the Transferor a full and sufficient indemnity but not further or otherwise hereby covenants with the Transferor that the Transferee and the persons deriving title under it will at all times hereafter observe and perform the covenants and conditions referred to in the Charges Register and keep the Transferor indemnified against all liability in respect of any further breach thereof so far as the same affect the property hereby transferred and are still subsisting and capable of being enforced

12. *The Transferors and all other necessary parties should execute this transfer as a deed using the space below*

THE COMMON SEAL of

[   ]

was hereunto affixed in the presence of:-

Director

Director/Secretary

Signed as a Deed by   )

[_____]   )

in the presence of:-   )

FORM 3

NOTICE PURSUANT TO THE PROVISIONS
OF THE LANDLORD AND TENANT ACT 1987
(AS AMENDED BY THE HOUSING ACT 1996) ('the Act')

Notice: Section 5B Notice by the Landlord to
                                     the Tenants in case of sale by auction

Property:
Tenure:
Headlease:
Landlord:
Landlord's Solicitors:
Title Number:
Principal Terms of Contract: To be sold subject to the Standard
                                    Conditions of Sale (Third Edition) and
                                    subject as set out below:—

1. The Landlord's interest is registered at HM Land Registry with the
    Title Number   .
2. The Property is sold with [Full/Limited] Title Guarantee and subject
    to all matters referred to in the registers of the Title Number other than
    charges to secure money.
3. [On completion of any transfer hereunder the Buyer shall pay to the
    Landlord the amount of arrears of ground rent service charge or other
    sums lawfully due to the Landlord in addition to the consideration.]

TAKE NOTICE THAT:

1. The Landlord proposes to dispose of its interest in the Property at an
    auction. This notice constitutes an offer by the Landlord which may be
    accepted by the requisite majority (over 50% of the qualifying tenants
    within the meaning of the Act) of qualifying tenants of the flats in the
    Property for the contract (if any) entered into by the Landlord at the
    auction to have effect as if a person or persons nominated by them,
    and not the purchaser, had entered into it.
2. This offer may be accepted within a period of two months and one day
    from the date of service of this notice. Unless you are given further
    notice to the contrary this notice will have been deemed to have been
    served within two days after posting by first class post to you or on the
    day after delivery if this notice has been delivered by hand.

3. On or before a date twenty nine days after the expiry of the date specified in paragraph 2 above you must nominate a person for the purpose of Section 6 of the Act into whose name the Property is to be transferred

ANY NOTICE TO BE SERVED ON THE LANDLORD IS TO BE SERVED UPON THE LANDLORD'S SOLICITORS

Signed ....

(As agent for the Landlord)

Dated ....

Notes

1. Section 3 of the Act: definition of a qualifying tenant.
2. Section 2 of the Act: definition of a landlord.
3. Section 18A of the Act: definition of the requisite majority which is more than 50 per cent of the available votes.
4. Section 5(1) and (3) of the Act: definition of the constituent flats which are the flats in the building.
5. Section 5B(8) states that unless the time and place of the auction and the name of the auctioneers are stated on this notice, the landlord must serve a further notice giving those particulars at least 28 days before the auction.

FORM 4

NOTICE PURSUANT TO THE PROVISIONS
OF THE LANDLORD AND TENANT ACT 1987
(AS AMENDED BY THE HOUSING ACT 1996) ('the Act')

Notice:

Section 5C Notice by the Landlord to the Tenants in case of grant of option or right of pre-emption

Property:
Tenure:
Headlease:
Landlord:
Landlord's Solicitors:
Title Number:
Consideration:

PLEASE TAKE NOTICE THAT:

1. This Notice constitutes an offer by the Landlord to grant [an option/a right of pre-emption] over the Property on the following terms which may be accepted by the requisite majority of qualifying tenants of the flats in the Property
    1.1   The amount payable to the Landlord is the Consideration
    1.2   The estate or interest to which the [option/right of pre-emption] relates is
    1.3   The consideration payable on exercise of the option or right of re-emption is
    1.4   The principal terms on which the [option/right of pre-emption] would be exercisable are
    1.5   The other principal terms of the disposal are
2. You may accept this offer within a period of two months and one day from the date of service of this notice unless you are given further notice to the contrary this notice will have been deemed to have been served within two days after posting by first class post to you or on the day after delivery if the notice has been delivered by hand.
3. Within a period of two months and one day from the expiry of the date specified in paragraph 2 above you must nominate a person or persons under Section 6 of the Act.

ANY NOTICE TO BE SERVED ON THE LANDLORD IS TO BE SERVED UPON THE LANDLORD'S SOLICITORS

Signed ....

(As agent for the Landlord)

Dated ....

Notes

1. Section 3 of the Act: definition of a qualifying tenant.
2. Section 2 of the Act: definition of a landlord.
3. Section 18A of the Act: definition of the requisite majority which is more than 50 per cent of the available votes.
4. Section 5(1) and (3) of the Act: definition of the constituent flats which are the flats in the building.

FORM 5
NOTICE PURSUANT TO THE PROVISIONS
OF THE LANDLORD AND TENANT ACT 1987
(AS AMENDED BY THE HOUSING ACT 1996) ('the Act')

Notice: Section 5D Notice by the Landlord to the Tenants in case of a conveyance not preceded by contract, option or right of pre-emption binding on the Landlord

Property:
Tenure:
Headlease:
Landlord:
Landlord's Solicitors:
Title Number:
Consideration:

PLEASE TAKE NOTICE THAT:

1. This Notice constitutes an offer by the Landlord to dispose of the Property on the following terms which may be accepted by the requisite majority of qualifying tenants of the flats in the Property
   1.1 The amount payable to the Landlord is the Consideration
   1.2 The estate or interest which the Landlord intends to dispose of is
   1.3 The other principal terms of the disposal are
2. You may accept this notice within a period of two months and one day from the date of service of this notice unless you are given further notice to the contrary this notice will have been deemed to have been served within two days after posting by first class post to you or on the day after delivery if the notice has been delivered by hand.
3. Within a period of two months and one day from the date a qualifying tenant is defined in Section 3 of the Act you must nominate a person or persons under Section 6 of the Act.

ANY NOTICE TO BE SERVED ON THE LANDLORD IS TO BE SERVED UPON THE LANDLORD'S SOLICITORS

Signed ....
(As agent for the Landlord)
Dated ....

Notes

1. Section 3 of the Act: definition of a qualifying tenant.
2. Section 2 of the Act: definition of a landlord.
3. Section 18A of the Act: definition of the requisite majority which is more than 50 per cent of the available votes.
4. Section 5(1) and (3) of the Act: definition of the constituent flats which are the flats in the building.

FORM 6

NOTICE PURSUANT TO THE PROVISIONS OF THE LANDLORD AND TENANT ACT 1987 (AS AMENDED BY THE HOUSING ACT 1996) ('the Act')

Notice:

Section 5E Notice by the Landlord to the Tenants in case of disposal for non-monetary consideration

Property:
Tenure:
Headlease:
Landlord:
Landlord's Solicitors:
Title Number:
Principal Terms of Contract:

To be sold subject to the Standard Conditions of Sale (Third Edition) and on the terms of the Agreement annexed hereto

PLEASE TAKE NOTICE THAT:

1. [Include relevant wording from Forms 5A, 5B, 5C or 5D whichever is applicable.]
2. Because the consideration required by the Landlord does not consist of money or does not wholly consist of money:
   2.1 The requisite majority of qualifying tenants may invoke an election under Section 8C of the Act. The effect of that election is to preserve the rights of the qualifying tenants. Provided the correct procedure is following those rights are then effective against any purchaser of the protected interest. Whatever part of the consideration did not consist of money may be given a value. That value can be fixed by a leasehold valuation tribunal.
   2.2 Accordingly, this notice also consitutes an offer by the Landlord to the requisite majority of qualifying tenants of constituent flats for a person or persons nominated by them to acquire the Property in pursuance of Section 11 to 17 of the Act.
   2.3 This offer may be accepted at any time before a date of two months and one day from the date of service of this notice.

ANY NOTICE TO BE SERVED ON THE LANDLORD IS TO BE SERVED UPON THE LANDLORD'S SOLICITORS

Signed ....

(As agent for the Landlord)

Dated ....

Notes

1. Section 3 of the Act: definition of a qualifying tenant.
2. Section 2 of the Act: definition of a landlord.
3. Section 18A of the Act: definition of the requisite majority which is more than 50 per cent of the available votes.
4. Section 5(1) and (3) of the Act: definition of the constituent flats which are the flats in the building.
5. Section 11(3) states that 'purchaser' means the transferee under the original disposal or (in a surrender) the superior landlord.
6. Section 20(1) states that the protected interest is the estate, interest or other subject-matter of this offer-notice.

FORM 7
NOTICE PURSUANT TO THE PROVISIONS
OF THE LANDLORD AND TENANT ACT 1987
(AS AMENDED BY THE HOUSING ACT 1996) ('the Act')

Notice: Section 6(3) Notice by the requisite
                                           majority of qualifying tenants of
                                           acceptance

Property:
Tenure:
Landlord:
Tenant's Solicitors:
Title Number:
Landlord's Notice:

PLEASE TAKE NOTICE THAT:

1. This Notice constitutes an acceptance by the requisite majority of the
    qualifying tenants of the constituent flats of the offer by the Landlord
    contained in the Landlord's Notice
2. The requisite majority of qualifying tenants of the constituent flats are
    as described in the schedule annexed hereto.
3. [The person who is duly nominated as the nominated person for the
    purposes of the Act is

    The nominated person to whom the Property should be transferred by
    you shall be advised to in accordance with the terms of the Landlord's
    Notice]*

*Delete as appropriate

THE SCHEDULE

ANY NOTICE TO BE SERVED ON THE QUALIFYING TENANTS IS TO BE SERVED UPON THE TENANT'S SOLICITORS

Signed ....

(As agent for the qualifying tenants)

Dated ....

Notes

1. Section 3 of the Act: definition of a qualifying tenant.
2. Section 2 of the Act: definition of a landlord.
3. Section 18A of the Act: definition of the requisite majority which is more than 50 per cent of the available votes.
4. Section 5(1) and (3) of the Act: definition of the constituent flats which are the flats in the building.

FORM 8

NOTICE PURSUANT TO THE PROVISIONS
OF THE LANDLORD AND TENANT ACT 1987
(AS AMENDED BY THE HOUSING ACT 1996) ('the Act')

Notice: Section 6(5) Notice by the qualifying
                                      tenants to the Landlord informing the
                                      Landlord of the Nominated Person

Property:
Tenure:
Landlord:
Landlord's Solicitors:
Landlord's Notice:
Tenant's Acceptance:
Title Number:

TAKE NOTICE THAT:

1. Under the Tenant's Acceptance the qualifying tenants did not specify
   the Nominated Person
2. The Nominated Person of the qualifying tenants for the purpose of
   this disposal is

ANY NOTICE TO BE SERVED ON THE QUALIFYING TENANTS IS
TO BE SERVED UPON THE TENANT'S SOLICITORS

Signed ....
(As agent for the qualifying tenants)
Dated ....

Notes

1. Section 2 of the Act: definition of a landlord.
2. Section 18A of the Act: definition of a qualifying tenant.
3. This form is to be used where the nominated person was not stated in
   the tenant's acceptance notice.

FORM 9

NOTICE PURSUANT TO THE PROVISIONS
OF THE LANDLORD AND TENANT ACT 1987
(AS AMENDED BY THE HOUSING ACT 1996) ('the Act')

Notice: Section 8(3)(a) Notice by the Landlord
                                     to the Nominated Person of with-
                                     drawal by the Landlord from the
                                     transaction

Property:
Tenure:
Landlord:
Landlord's Solicitors:
Title Number:
Date of Landlord's Notice:
Date of Tenant's Acceptance:
Nominated Person:

PLEASE TAKE NOTICE THAT:

1. This Notice constitutes a notice by the Landlord to the Nominated
    Person that the Landlord does not wish to proceed with the disposal
    of the Property to the Nominated Person.
2. This does not prejudice the application of Part I of the Act to any
    further offer notice served by the Landlord on the qualifying tenants
    of the flats in the building.

ANY NOTICE TO BE SERVED ON THE LANDLORD IS TO BE
SERVED UPON THE LANDLORD'S SOLICITORS

Signed ....
(As agent for the Landlord)
Dated ....

Notes

1. Section 2 of the Act: definition of a landlord.
2. Section 3 of the Act: definition of a qualifying tenant.
3. Section 18A of the Act: requisite majority is more than 50 per cent of
    the available votes.

FORM 10

NOTICE PURSUANT TO THE PROVISIONS
OF THE LANDLORD AND TENANT ACT 1987
(AS AMENDED BY THE HOUSING ACT 1996) ('the Act')

Notice:	Section 8A(4)(a) Notice by the Nominated Person to the Landlord of withdrawal by the Nominated Person from the transaction

Property:
Tenure:
Landlord:
Tenant's Solicitors:
Title Number:
Landlord's Notice:
Tenant's Acceptance:
Nominated Person:

PLEASE TAKE NOTICE THAT:

This Notice constitutes a notice by the Nominated Person to the Landlord that the Nominated Person does not wish to proceed with the acquisition of the Property from the Landlord as offered by the Landlord's Notice and accepted by the Tenant's Acceptance.

ANY NOTICE TO BE SERVED ON THE NOMINATED PERSON IS TO

BE SERVED UPON THE TENANT'S SOLICITORS

Signed ....
(As agent for the Nominated Person)
Dated ....

Note

Section 2 of the Act: definition of a landlord.

FORM 11

NOTICE PURSUANT TO THE PROVISIONS
OF THE LANDLORD AND TENANT ACT 1987
(AS AMENDED BY THE HOUSING ACT 1996) ('the Act')

Notice: Section 8B(2) Notice by the
                                           Nominated Person to the Landlord
                                           of acceptance of the provisions of
                                           Section 8B

Property:
Tenure:
Landlord:
Tenant's Solicitors:
Title Number:
Landlord's Notice:
Tenant's Acceptance:
Nominated Person:
Date of Auction:

PLEASE TAKE NOTICE THAT:

This Notice constitutes a notice by the Nominated Person to the Landlord
that the Nominated Person elects that the provisions of Section 8B of the
Act shall apply

ANY NOTICE TO BE SERVED ON THE NOMINATED PERSON IS TO
BE SERVED UPON THE TENANT'S SOLICITORS

Signed ....
(As agent for the Nominated Person)
Dated ....

Note

Section 2 of the Act: definition of a landlord.

FORM 12

NOTICE PURSUANT TO THE PROVISIONS
OF THE LANDLORD AND TENANT ACT 1987
(AS AMENDED BY THE HOUSING ACT 1996) ('the Act')

Notice: Section 8B(4)(a) Notice by the
                                            Nominated Person to the Landlord of
                                            acceptance of the terms of the auction
                                            contract

Property:
Tenure:
Landlord:
Tenant's Solicitors:
Title Number:
Landlord's Notice:
Tenant's Acceptance:
Nominated Person:
Date of Auction:

PLEASE TAKE NOTICE THAT:

This Notice constitutes a notice by the Nominated Person to the Landlord
that the Nominated Person accepts the terms of the auction

**ANY NOTICE TO BE SERVED ON THE NOMINATED PERSON IS TO
BE SERVED UPON THE TENANT'S SOLICITORS**

Signed ....
(As agent for the qualifying tenants)
Dated ....

Note

Section 2 of the Act: definition of a landlord.

FORM 13

NOTICE PURSUANT TO THE PROVISIONS
OF THE LANDLORD AND TENANT ACT 1987
(AS AMENDED BY THE HOUSING ACT 1996) ('the Act')

Notice: Section 8C(2) Notice by the requisite
                                         majority of qualifying tenants of
                                         acceptance of an offer of disposal for
                                         non-monetary consideration

Property:
Tenure:
Landlord:
Tenant's Solicitors:
Title Number:
Landlord's Notice:

PLEASE TAKE NOTICE THAT:

1. This Notice constitutes an acceptance by the requisite majority of the
    qualifying tenants of the Flats in the Property that the provisions of
    Section 8C of the Act shall apply
2. The requisite majority of qualifying tenants of the constituent flats are
    as described in the schedule annexed hereto.
3. [The person who is duly nominated as the nominated person for the
    purposes of the Act is

    The nominated person to whom the Property should be transferred by
    you shall be advised to in accordance with the terms of the Landlord's
    Notice]*

*Delete as appropriate

THE SCHEDULE

ANY NOTICE TO BE SERVED ON THE QUALIFYING TENANTS IS TO BE SERVED UPON THE TENANT'S SOLICITORS

Signed ....
(As agent for the qualifying tenants)
Dated ....

Notes

1. Section 3 of the Act: definition of a qualifying tenant.
2. Section 2 of the Act: definition of a landlord.
3. Section 18A of the Act: definition of the requisite majority which is more than 50 per cent of the available votes.
4. Section 5(1) and (3) of the Act: definition of the constituent flats which are the flats in the building.

FORM 14

NOTICE PURSUANT TO THE PROVISIONS
OF THE LANDLORD AND TENANT ACT 1987
(AS AMENDED BY THE HOUSING ACT 1996) ('the Act')

Notice:

Section 8E(3) Notice by the Landlord to the Nominated Person stating that the Landlord has discharged its duty under Section 8E of the Act

Property:
Tenure:
Landlord:
Landlord's Solicitors:
Title Number:
Landlord's Notice:
Tenant's Acceptance:
Nominated Person

PLEASE TAKE NOTICE THAT:

1. By virtue of the Tenant's Acceptance the Landlord is obliged to proceed with the disposal of the Property a per the Landlord's Notice.
2. The Landlord is however precluded from proceeding by a covenant condition or other obligation unless the consent of some other person is obtained.
3. The Landlord has to use its best endeavours to secure that the consent of that person to this disposal is given.
4. As it appeared to the landlord that that person cannot unreasonably withhold consent, the Landlord instigated proceedings to obtain a declaration to that effect.
5. As the Landlord cannot obtain that person's consent and cannot obtain a declaration to that effect the Landlord hereby notifies the Nominated Person that the above is the case.

ANY NOTICE TO BE SERVED ON THE LANDLORD IS TO BE SERVED UPON THE LANDLORD'S SOLICITORS

Signed ....
(As agent for the Landlord)
Dated ....

Note

Section 2 of the Act: definition of a landlord.

FORM 15
NOTICE PURSUANT TO THE PROVISIONS OF THE LANDLORD AND TENANT ACT 1987 (AS AMENDED BY THE HOUSING ACT 1996) ('the Act')

Notice: Section [9A(1) and 14(1)] Notice by the
                                          Nominated Person to the Landlord of
                                          withdrawal by the Nominated Person
                                          from the transaction

Property:
Tenure:
Landlord:
Tenant's Solicitors:
Title Number:
Landlord's Notice:
Tenant's Acceptance:
Nominated Person:

PLEASE TAKE NOTICE THAT:

This Notice constitutes a notice by the Nominated Person to the Landlord
that the Nominated Person does not wish to proceed with the aquisition
of the Property from the Landlord.

**ANY NOTICE TO BE SERVED ON THE NOMINATED PERSON IS TO
BE SERVED UPON THE TENANT'S SOLICITORS**

Signed ....

(As agent for the Nominated Person)

Dated ....

Notes

1. A landlord is defined in s. 2 of the Act.
2. This notice can be served under either s. 9A or s. 14.

FORM 16

NOTICE PURSUANT TO THE PROVISIONS
OF THE LANDLORD AND TENANT ACT 1987
(AS AMENDED BY THE HOUSING ACT 1996) ('the Act')

Notice: Section 9B(1) Notice by the Landlord
                                           to the Nominated Person of with-
                                           drawal

Property:
Tenure:
Landlord:
Landlord's Solicitors:
Title Number:

TAKE NOTICE THAT:

The Landlord does not wish to proceed with the disposal of the Property

**ANY NOTICE TO BE SERVED ON THE LANDLORD IS TO BE
SERVED UPON THE LANDLORD'S SOLICITORS**

Signed ....
(As agent for the Landlord)
Dated ....

Note

Section 2 of the Act: definition of a landlord.

FORM 17

NOTICE PURSUANT TO THE PROVISIONS
OF THE LANDLORD AND TENANT ACT 1987
(AS AMENDED BY THE HOUSING ACT 1996) ('the Act')

Notice: Section 10(1) Notice by the Landlord
                                               to the qualifying tenants stating that
                                               the Property has ceased to be within
                                               the Act

Property:
Tenure:
Landlord:
Landlord's Solicitors:
Title Number:
Landlord's Notice:

PLEASE TAKE NOTICE THAT:

This Notice constitutes a notice by the Landlord to the qualifying tenants
of the constituent flats staring that the Property has ceased to be premises
to which Part I of the Act applies and that the Landlord's Notice and
anything done in pursuance of it is to be treated as not having been served
or done

ANY NOTICE TO BE SERVED ON THE LANDLORD IS TO BE
SERVED UPON THE LANDLORD'S SOLICITORS

Signed ....
(As agent for the Landlord)
Dated ....

Notes

1. Section 3 of the Act: definition of a qualifying tenant.
2. Section 2 of the Act: definition of a landlord.
3. Section 18A of the Act: definition of the requisite majority which is
    more than 50 per cent of the available votes.
4. Section 5(1) and (3) of the Act: definition of the constituent flats which
    are the flats in the building.

FORM 18
NOTICE PURSUANT TO THE PROVISIONS
OF THE LANDLORD AND TENANT ACT 1987
(AS AMENDED BY THE HOUSING ACT 1996) ('the Act')

Notice:

Section 11A(1) Notice by the requisite majority of qualifying tenants to a purchaser

Property:
Purchaser:
Tenant's Solicitors:

PLEASE TAKE NOTICE THAT:

1. This Notice constitutes a notice by the requisite majority of the qualifying tenants of the constituent flats to you the Purchaser of the Property requiring you:
   - 1.1 to give particulars of the terms on which the disposal to you of the Property by the Landlord was made (including the deposit and consideration required) and the date on which it was made, and
   - 1.2 where the disposal consisted of entering into a contract, to provide a copy of the contract
2. The above particulars are to be given, or the copy of the contract provided, to the Tenant's Solicitors on behalf of the qualifying tenants
3. This notice will have been deemed to be served within two days after posting by first class post to you or on the day after delivery if delivered by hand
4. You have one month to comply with this notice beginning with the date on which it is served on you

ANY NOTICE TO BE SERVED ON THE QUALIFYING TENANTS IS
TO BE SERVED UPON THE TENANT'S SOLICITORS

Signed ....
(As agent for the qualifying tenants)
Dated ....

Notes

1. Section 3 of the Act: definition of a qualifying tenant.
2. Section 2 of the Act: definition of a landlord.

3. Section 18A of the Act: definition of the requisite majority which is more than 50 per cent of the available votes.

4. Section 5(1) and (3) of the Act: definition of the constituent flats which are the flats in the building.

FORM 19

NOTICE PURSUANT TO THE PROVISIONS
OF THE LANDLORD AND TENANT ACT 1987
(AS AMENDED BY THE HOUSING ACT 1996) ('the Act')

Notice:

Section 12A Notice by the requisite majority of qualifying tenants to the Landlord

Property:
Landlord:
Purchaser:
Tenant's Solicitors:
Contract:
Nominated Person:

PLEASE TAKE NOTICE THAT:

1. You have previously entered into the Contract with the Purchaser for the disposal of the Property
2. [This Notice constitutes a notice by the requisite majority of the qualifying tenants of the constituent flats to you the Landlord to elect that the Contract shall have effect as if not entered into with the Purchaser but with the Nominated Person][a]

   [This Notice constitutes a notice by the requisite majority of the qualifyng tenants of the constituent flats to you the Landlord to elect that the estate or interest specified in the schedule hereto be transferred to the qualifying tenants in the terms therein certified][b]

   [This Notice constitutes a notice by the requisite majority of the qualifyng tenants of the constituent flats to you the Landlord to elect that the part of the property to which at the date of the original disposal Part I of the Act applied to be transferred to the qualifying tenants and for that property and the forms of the transfer to be determined by a Leasehold Valuation Tribunal][c]
3. This notice will have been deemed to be served within two days after posting by first class post to you or on the day after delivery if delivered by hand

ANY NOTICE TO BE SERVED ON THE QUALIFYING TENANTS IS TO BE SERVED UPON THE TENANT'S SOLICITORS

Signed ....
(As agent for the qualifying tenants)
Dated ....

THE SCHEDULE

Notes

1. Section 3 of the Act: definition of a qualifying tenant.
2. Section 2 of the Act: definition of a landlord.
3. Section 18A of the Act: definition of the requisite majority which is more than 50 per cent of the available votes.
4. Section 5(1) and (3) of the Act: definition of the constituent flats which are the flats in the building.
5. Clause 2 contains three alternatives *a*, *b* and *c*. Alternative *a* is used when the tenants require a transfer of all the property in the original disposal and the Act applies to it all. If the Act did not apply to all the property in the original disposal then s. 12B(4) applies – the tenants may specify the part of the property of which they require a transfer (alternative *b*) or require it to be decided by a leasehold valuation tribunal (alternative *c*).

FORM 20
NOTICE PURSUANT TO THE PROVISIONS
OF THE LANDLORD AND TENANT ACT 1987
(AS AMENDED BY THE HOUSING ACT 1996) ('the Act')

Notice: Section 12B(2) Purchase Notice
Property:
Landlord:
Purchaser:
Tenant's Solicitors:
Contract:
Nominated Person:

PLEASE TAKE NOTICE THAT:

1. You have previously entered into the Contract for the disposal of the Property

2. This Notice constitutes a notice by the requisite majority of the qualifying tenants of the constituent flats to you the Purchaser requiring you to dispose of

    [the estate or interest that was the subject matter of the original disposal, on the terms on which it was made (including those relating to consideration payable) to the Nominated Person][a]

    [the estate or interest specified in the schedule hereto in the terms therein certified][b]

    [the part of the property to which at the date of the original disposal Part I of the Act applied and for that property and the forms of the transfer to be determined by a Leasehold Valuation Tribunal][c]

3. This notice will have been deemed to be served within two days after posting by first class post to you or on the day after delivery if delivered by hand

ANY NOTICE TO BE SERVED ON THE QUALIFYING TENANTS IS
TO BE SERVED UPON THE TENANT'S SOLICITORS

Signed ....
(As agent for the qualifying tenants)
Dated ....

Notes

1. A qualifying tenant is defined in s. 3 of the Act.
2. A landlord is defined in s. 2 of the Act.
3. The requisite majority is more than 50 per cent of the available votes: s. 18A.
4. The constituent flats are the flats in the building: s. 5(1) and (3).
5. Clause 2 contains three alternatives *a, b* and *c*. Alternative *a* is used when the tenants require a transfer of all the property in the original disposal and the Act applies to it all. If the Act did not apply to all the property in the original disposal then s. 12B(4) applies – the tenants may specify the part of the property of which they require a transfer (alternative *b*) or require it to be decided by a leasehold valuation tribunal (alternative *c*).

FORM 21
NOTICE PURSUANT TO THE PROVISIONS
OF THE LANDLORD AND TENANT ACT 1987
(AS AMENDED BY THE HOUSING ACT 1996) ('the Act')

Notice: Section 12C(2) Notice by the requisite majority of qualifying tenants to a purchaser requiring new tenancy

Property:
Purchaser:
Relevant Tenancy:
Tenant's Solicitors:
Nominated Person:

PLEASE TAKE NOTICE THAT:

1. This Notice constitues a notice by the requisite majority of the qualifying tenants of the constituent flats to you the purchaser of the Property requiring you to grant a new tenancy of the Property on the same terms as those of the Relevant Tenancy to the Nominated Person
2. This notice will have been deemed to be served within two days after posting by first class post to you or on the day after delivery if delivered by hand

**ANY NOTICE TO BE SERVED ON THE QUALIFYING TENANTS IS
TO BE SERVED UPON THE TENANT'S SOLICITORS**

Signed ....
(As agent for the qualifying tenants)
Dated ....

Notes

1. Section 3 of the Act: definition of a qualifying tenant.
2. Section 11(3) of the Act: definition of a purchaser.
3. Section 18A of the Act: definition of the requisite majority which is more than 50 per cent of the available votes.
4. Section 5(1) and (3) of the Act: definition of the constituent flats which are the flats in the building.

FORM 22

NOTICE PURSUANT TO THE PROVISIONS
OF THE LANDLORD AND TENANT ACT 1987
(AS AMENDED BY THE HOUSING ACT 1996) ('the Act')

Notice: Section 16(3)(a) Notice by the Pur-
                                           chaser to the Subsequent Purchaser
Property:
Purchaser:
Subsequent Purchaser:
Purchaser's Solicitors:

PLEASE TAKE NOTICE THAT:

There is annexed to this Notice a notice which has been served on the
Purchaser under section [12A/12B/12C]*

**ANY NOTICE TO BE SERVED ON THE PURCHASER IS TO BE
SERVED UPON THE PURCHASER'S SOLICITORS**

Signed ....
(As agent for the Purchaser)
Dated ....

*Delete as appropriate

FORM 23
NOTICE PURSUANT TO THE PROVISIONS
OF THE LANDLORD AND TENANT ACT 1987
(AS AMENDED BY THE HOUSING ACT 1996) ('the Act')

Notice: Section 16(3)(b) Notice by the Pur-
                                          chaser to the Nominated Person

Property:
Purchaser:
Subsequent Purchaser:
Purchaser's Solicitors:
Nominated Person:

PLEASE TAKE NOTICE THAT:

The Purchaser has disposed of its interest to the Subsequent Purchaser

**ANY NOTICE TO BE SERVED ON THE PURCHASER IS TO BE
SERVED UPON THE PURCHASER'S SOLICITORS**

Signed ....
(As agent for the Purchaser)
Dated ....

FORM 24
NOTICE PURSUANT TO THE PROVISIONS
OF THE LANDLORD AND TENANT ACT 1987
(AS AMENDED BY THE HOUSING ACT 1996) ('the Act')

Notice: Section 16(2)(a) Notice by the Pur-
                                            chaser to the Tenants

Property:
Purchaser:
Purchaser's Solicitors:
Subsequent Purchaser:
Tenant's Notice:

PLEASE TAKE NOTICE THAT:

1. By virtue of the Tenant's Notice the Purchaser is required to provide
    to the qualifying tenants who served the Tenant's Notice details of to
    whom the Purchaser has disposed of the Purchaser's interest in the
    Property.
2. The Purchaser has disposed of its interest in the Property to the
    Subsequent Purchaser.

**ANY NOTICE TO BE SERVED ON THE PURCHASER IS TO BE
SERVED UPON THE PURCHASER'S SOLICITORS**

Signed ....

(As agent for the Purchaser)

Dated ....

Notes

1. Section 2 of the Act: definition of a landlord.
2. Section 11(3) states that 'purchaser' means the transferee under the
    original disposal or (if a surrender) the superior landlord.
3. The purchaser has to reply to the earlier s. 11A notice and that
    reply can and usually will contain those particulars. There will be
    a s. 16(2)(b) notice served on the subsequent purchaser.

FORM 25

NOTICE PURSUANT TO THE PROVISIONS
OF THE LANDLORD AND TENANT ACT 1987
(AS AMENDED BY THE HOUSING ACT 1996) ('the Act')

Notice: Section 17 Notice by the Purchaser to
                                          the Tenants that Act has ceased to
                                          apply

Property:
Tenure:
Purchaser:
Purchaser's Solicitors:
Title Number:

PLEASE TAKE NOTICE THAT:

This Notice constitutes a notice by the Purchaser to the qualifying tenants
of the constituent flats stating that the Property has ceased to be premises
to which Part I of the Act applies and that the notice served on him and
anything done in pursuance of it is to be treated as not having been served
or done.

**ANY NOTICE TO BE SERVED ON THE PURCHASER IS TO BE
SERVED UPON THE PURCHASER'S SOLICITORS**

Signed ....
(As agent for the Purchaser)
Dated ....

Notes

1. Section 2 of the Act: definition of a landlord.
2. Section 11(3) states that 'purchaser' means the transferee under the
    original disposal or (if a surrender) the superior landlord.
3. The purchaser has to reply to the earlier s. 11A notice and that
    reply can and usually will contain those particulars. There will be
    a s. 16(2)(b) notice.

FORM 26

NOTICE PURSUANT TO THE PROVISIONS
OF THE LANDLORD AND TENANT ACT 1987
(AS AMENDED BY THE HOUSING ACT 1996) ('the Act')

Notice: Section 5B(8) Notice by the Landlord
                                           informing the Tenants of the particu-
                                           lars of the auction

Property:
Tenure:
Headlease:
Landlord:
Landlord's Solicitors:
Title Number:

PLEASE TAKE NOTICE THAT:

Date of offer notice sent to you:
Date of auction:
Place of auction:
Time of auction:
Auctioneers:

ANY NOTICE TO BE SERVED ON THE LANDLORD IS TO BE
SERVED UPON THE LANDLORD'S SOLICITORS

Signed ....
(As agent for the Landlord)
Dated ....

FORM 27

NOTICE PURSUANT TO THE PROVISIONS
OF THE LANDLORD AND TENANT ACT 1987
(AS AMENDED BY THE HOUSING ACT 1996) ('the Act')

Notice: Section 18(1) Notice by the Prospec-
                                         tive Purchaser to the qualifying ten-
                                         ants

Property :
Title Number:
Prospective Purchaser:
Prospective Purchaser's Solicitors:
Landlord:
Consideration:

PLEASE TAKE NOTICE THAT:

1. This notice is given under the provisions of the Landlord and Tenant
    Act 1987 section 18(1) and relates to the Property in which the flat of
    which you are a tenant is situated being the premises registered at HM
    Land Registry with the Title Number

2. The Landlord owns the freehold of the Property and proposes to make
    a disposal of the Property to the Prospective Purchaser for the
    consideration

3. WE NOW INVITE YOU to serve a notice pursuant to the Landlord
    and Tenant Act 1987 section 18(2)(b) on us as agents for the Prospec-
    tive Purchaser stating:

    3.1 whether the Landlord has served on you or any predecessor in
         title of yours a notice under the Landlord and Tenant Act 1987
         section 5 in respect of the proposed disposal;

    3.2 if the Landlord has not so served any such notice, whether you
         are aware of any reason why you were not entitled to be served
         with any such notice by the Landlord;

    3.3 if you are not so aware, whether you would wish to avail yourself
         to the right of first refusal conferred by any such notice if it were
         served.

4. In accordance with the Landlord and Tenant Act 1987 section 18 WE
    INFORM YOU that where the Prospective Purchaser has served
    notices such as this on at least 80 per cent of the tenants of the flats
    affected by the proposed disposal and:

    4.1 not more than 50 per cent of the tenants on whom those notices
         have been served by the Prospective Purchaser have served

notices in pursuance of the Landlord and Tenant Act 1987 section 18(2)(b) by the end of the period of two months beginning with the date on which the last of them was served with a notice under Section 18 of that Act; or

4.2 more than 50 per cent of the tenants on whom those notices have been served by the Prospective Purchaser have served notices in pursuance of the Landlord and Tenant Act 1987 section 18(2)(b) but the notices in each case indicate that the tenant serving it either:

4.2.1 does not regard himself as being entitled to be served by the Landlord with a notice under the Landlord and Tenant Act 1987 section 5 in respect of the proposed disposal, or

4.2.2 would not wish to avail himself of the right of first refusal conferred by such a notice if it were served;

The Property will, in relation to the proposed disposal, be treated for the purposes of the Landlord and Tenant Act 1987 Part I as premises to which Part I of the Act does not apply.

5. For the purposes of the Landlord and Tenant Act 1987 section 18(3) each of the flats affected is to be regarded as having one tenant only to count towards the percentages above whether that tenant is a qualifying tenant or not.

6. If you and other qualifying tenants wish to respond to this notice, notices in pursuance of the Landlord and Tenant Act 1987 section 18(2)(b) must be served by the end of the period of two months beginning with the latest date on which a notice in this form is served [and notices are being served on all tenants in the Property today]. If the steps required by the Landlord and Tenant Act 1987 are not taken within that period of two months, the disposal to the Prospective Purchaser may proceed without Part I of that Act applying.

7. The information requested in response to this notice and all correspondence about this notice should be sent to us as agents for the Prospective Purchaser at the address given above.

Any notice to be served on the Prospective Purchaser is to be served on the Prospective Purchaser's Solicitors.

Signed ....

(As agent for the Prospective Purchaser)

Dated this   day of   1999

The Corresponding Date Rule

CALCULATION OF TIME: THE CORRESPONDING DATE RULE

Dodds v *Walker* [1981] 1 WLR 1027; [1981] 2 All ER 609

This rule is stated by Lord Russell as follows:

> It is common ground that ordinarily the calculation of a period of a calendar month or calendar months ends on what has been conveniently referred to as the corresponding date. For example, in a four-month period, when service of the relevant notice was on 28th September, time would begin to run at midnight 28th–29th September and would end at midnight 28th–29th January, a period embracing four calendar months. It is to be observed that the number of days in the four-month period in that example is in one sense inevitable limited by the fact that September and November each contains but 30 days. But the application of the corresponding date principle inevitably produces variation in the number of days involved, depending on the date on which a four-month notice is served and the irregular allotment of days to different months. Sometimes it is not possible to apply directly the principle, for instance if a four-month notice is served on 30th October (the time beginning to run at midnight 30th–31st October), there being in February but 28 (or 29) days it is not possible to find a corresponding date in February and plainly a corresponding date cannot be sought in

March; the application of the corresponding date principle in such case can only lead to termination of the four-month period at midnight 28th February–1st March (or midnight 29th February–1st March in a leap year).

Landlord and Tenant Act 1985, s. 3A

3A. Duty to inform tenant of possible right to acquire landlord's interest

(1)   Where a new landlord is required by section 3(1) to give notice to a tenant of an assignment to him, then if—

(a)   the tenant is a qualifying tenant within the meaning of Part I of the Landlord and Tenant Act 1987 (tenants' rights of first refusal), and

(b)   the assignment was a relevant disposal within the meaning of that Part affecting premises to which at the time of the disposal that Part applied,

the landlord shall give also notice in writing to the tenant to the following effect.

(2)   The notice shall state—

(a)   that the disposal to the landlord was one to which Part I of the Landlord and Tenant Act 1987 applied;

(b)   that the tenant (together with other qualifying tenants) may have the right under that Part—

(i)   to obtain information about the disposal, and

(ii)   to acquire the landlord's interest in the whole or part of the premises in which the tenant's flat is situated; and

(c)   the time within which any such right must be exercised, and the fact that the time would run from the date of receipt of notice under this section by the requisite majority of qualifying tenants (within the meaning of that Part).

(3)　A person who is required to give notice under this section and who fails, without reasonable excuse, to do so within the time allowed for giving notice under section 3(1) commits a summary offence and is liable on conviction to a fine not exceeding level 4 on the standard scale.

Index

Acceptance of offer
  auction contract   131
  non-monetary consideration   132–3
  notice   125–6, 130–3
  protected period   29–30
    extension   30
    injunction to prevent breach   29–30
  s. 6 procedures   30
Application of Act   1–19
  contracts   17
  disposals *see* Disposals
  land associated with building   7
  landlord *see* Landlords
  options *see* Options
  pre-emption rights *see* Pre-emption rights
  premises *see* Premises
  qualifying tenant *see* Qualifying tenants
  sub-sales   12
  sub-tenancies   11–12
Appurtenances   4, 43–5
  precarious   58
Assignment covenants
  absolute covenants   36
  disposal constrained by   35–6
  notice   36, 134
  qualified covenants   36
Associated company disposals   17, 56
Assured agricultural occupancy   13–14
Assured tenancy   13–14
Auction sale
  nominated persons obligations   35, 131
  notice of particulars   149

Auction sale — *continued*
  offer notice   24–6, 32, 117–18
  premises   10
  public   25, 26
  timescale for public sales   25, 26
Avoidance of Act
  company schemes   56
  conditional contracts   56
  s. 18 procedure   57
  security document use   56–7

Buildings
  appurtenances   4, 43–5, 58
    precarious   58
  common parts   8
  divided horizontally from some other part
    of   6
  land associated with   7
  meaning   3–4
  mixed use   7–8
  more than one   9–10
  part of   5
  several   20–2, 57
  severance
    service charge   21–2
    title problems   22
Business tenancy exception   13

Cessation notice   37, 137
Change in value   47
Common parts
  disposal   57–8

Common parts — *continued*
  floor area   8
Companies
  associated   17, 56
  criminal offences by officers   55
  in liquidation   15
Company schemes   56
Compulsory purchase orders   16
Contract
  application of Act   17
  binding nature   36–7
  C(iv) land charge   37
  conditional   56
  conveyance not preceded by
    27, 121–2
  exchange   35
  failure to act, nominated person   34
  failure to provide   33
  landlord's obligation to send   33
  taking benefit of
    appurtenant land   43–5
    more than one building   42–3
    premises   42–3
    right   42
    rights over other land   43–5
    sports facilities   44–5
Corresponding date rule   33, 152–3
Costs
  leasehold valuation tribunal   61
  nominated person   35, 41
County court
  jurisdiction   61–2
  Order 43   62
  originating proceedings   62
  special jurisdiction procedure   62
Criminal offences
  by officers of body corporate   55
  effect on disposal   55–6
  failure to comply with requirements
    54
  prosecutors   55
  reasonable excuse defence   54–5
Crown, disposals to   16

Discharge of incumbrances   46–7
Disposals
  in 12-month period   32
  associated company   17, 56
  by purchaser *see* Purchasers
  common parts   57–8
  company in liquidation   15
  compulsory purchase orders   16
  constrained by assignment
    covenants   35–6
    notice   36, 134

Disposals — *continued*
  criminal offence effect   55–6
  excepted   15–17
  family provisions   15–16
  foreclosure   56–7
  incorporeal hereditaments   15
  involuntary   15–16
  non-monetary consideration
    28, 123–4, 132–3
  obligations created before commencement
    of Act   17
  options   16, 18–19, 26–7, 119–20
  pre-emption rights   16, 18–19, 26–7,
    119–20
  relevant   14
  securities   15
  Settled Land Act beneficiary interests
    15
  several buildings   20–2, 57
  structured   57–8
  surrender of tenancy   16
  tenants taking over benefit   40, 140–1
  to Crown   16
  trustees in bankruptcy   15
  undervalue conveyances   16
  see also Protected period

Enforcement of Act   53
Exchange of contract   35
  failure to complete   35

Family
  provision, disposals and   15–16
  undervalue transactions   16
Floor areas   8
Foreclosure   56–7

Gardens   44–5

Hereditaments, incorporeal   15
High Court
  jurisdiction   62
  service of notice   62

Inaction by tenant   50–1
Incorporeal hereditaments   15
Incumbrances, discharge   46–7
Information right   38–9
  notice requesting   38, 138–9
Injunction remedy   29–30
Involuntary disposals
  company in liquidation   15
  compulsory purchase orders   16
  family provisions   15–16
  trustees in bankruptcy   15

Jurisdiction
  county court   61–2
  High Court   62

Land
  associated with building   7
  held under different titles   8–9
  transfer to nominated person   12
Landlord and Tenant Act 1985, s. 3A   39
  text   154–5
Landlord and Tenant Act 1987, text   63–102
Landlords   11
  contract
    failure to provide   33
    obligation to send   33
  exempt   58
  failure to complete exchange   35
  identification   2, 11
  immediate   2
  lapse of offer   37, 137
  notice of withdrawal   33, 128
  service of notices   23
  surrender by   47–8, 138–9
  withdrawal   33, 128
Lapse of offer   37, 137
Leasehold valuation tribunal   48–9, 59–60
  costs   61
  description   60
  jurisdiction   48–9, 59–60
  procedure for application   60–1
  questions for determination   60

Management company   40, 41

New tenancy, notice to purchaser requiring
  144
Nominated person
  contract to   33
  costs against   35, 41
  definition   31
  failure of tenants to make nomination   32
  failure to act   34
  landlord's failure to send contract to   33
  more than one   41
  nomination process   31–2
  procedure after nomination   33
  replacement   40
  response to contract   34
  transfer of land to   12
  withdrawal
    cost consequences   35
    notice   34, 129, 135
Non-monetary consideration
  acceptance of offer   132–3
  offer notice (s. 5E)   28, 123–4

Notices
  cessation notice   37, 137
  offer notices see Offer notice; S. 5 notices
  prospective purchaser   51–2, 148, 150–1
  purchase see Purchase notice
  qualified assignment covenants   36, 134
  s. 12A notices   42–5
  s. 12B notices   45–7
  s. 12C notices   47–8, 144
  service see Service of notices
  see also subject matter of individual notice
Nugee Report   1

Offer
  lapse   37, 137
  withdrawal see Withdrawal
Offer notice
  contract to create or transfer land
    (s. 5A)   24, 103–16
  conveyance not preceded by contract
    (s. 5D)   27, 121–2
  disposal of several buildings   20–2
  disposals possible   32
  non-monetary consideration (s. 5E)
    28, 123–4
  option or right of pre-emption grant
    (s. 5C)   26–7, 119–20
  requirement   20
  sale by auction   24–6, 32, 35, 117–18, 131
  service   22–3
    landlord's   23
    method   23
    time   23
Options
  application of Act   16, 18–19
  offer notice   26–7, 119–20
Overriding interest   53

Pre-emption rights   1
  application of Act   16, 18–19
  offer notice   26–7, 119–20
Premises
  appurtenances   4, 43–5
    precarious   58
  buildings
    common parts   8, 57
    divided horizontally from some other
      part of   6
    land associated with   7
    meaning   3–4
    mixed use   7–8
    more than one   9–10
    part of   5
    several   20–2, 57
    severance

Premises — *continued*
    service charge   21–2
    title problems   22
    see also appurtenances
  cessation notice   37, 137
  common parts   8, 57–8
  constructed or adapted for dwelling   5–6
  flats held by qualifying tenants
    number   6–7
    two or more   5–6
  land
    associated with building   7
    different titles   8–9
    transfer to nominated person   12
  let as separate dwelling   6
  meaning   4
  no longer qualifying   50, 146
  part of building   5
  separate set of premises   5
  to which Act applies   2–6
  whole or part of building   3–4
Property rights   53
Prospective purchaser notice
  51–2, 148, 150–1
Protected period   29–30, 32
  extension   30
  injunction to prevent breach   29–30
Purchase notice   45, 46, 142–3
  change in value of property   47
  content   47
  discharge of incumbrances   46–7
  s. 12A notices   42–5
Purchasers
  disposal of part   50
  exercise of tenants' rights against   41
  information rights   38–9
    compliance   39–40
  notice requiring new tenancy   144
  notice to subsequent purchaser
    49–50, 145
  notice to tenants   147
  prospective, notice   51–2, 148, 150–1
  right to compel sale   45, 142–3
  subsequent *see* Subsequent purchasers
  termination of rights against
    inaction by tenants   50–1
    no longer qualifying premises   50, 146

Qualifying tenants   2, 13–14
  assured agricultural occupancy   13–14
  assured tenancy   13–14
  business tenancies   13
  exceptions   12–14
  exercising rights   41
  failure to make nomination   32

Qualifying tenants — *continued*
  inaction   50–1
  information right   38–9
  multiple flat holders   14
  nominated person *see* Nominated person
  notice requesting information
    38, 138–9
  number of flats held by   6–7
  protected shorthold tenancy   12–13
  requisite majority
    acceptance notice   125–6, 132–3
    identification   31
    less than   34
      withdrawal necessary   34
    meaning   31
    number of votes   31
  right to compel sale by purchaser
    change in value of property   47
    content of notice   47
    discharge of incumbrances   46–7
    purchase notice   45, 46, 142–3
  service occupancies   13
  sub-tenancies   11–12
  two or more flats held by   5–6

Reasonable excuse defence   54–5
Requisite majority
  acceptance notice   125–6, 132–3
  identification   31
  less than   34
    withdrawal necessary   34
  meaning   31
  number of votes   31
'Right of pre-emption' *see* Pre-emption
  rights

Section 5 notices   18
  s. 5A   24, 103–16
  s. 5B   24–6, 32, 117–18
  s. 5C   26–7, 119–20
  s. 5D   27, 121–2
  s. 5E   28, 123–4
  see also Offer notice
Securities   15
Security documents   56–7
Service charge   21–2
Service occupancies   13
Service of notices
  High Court   62
  landlord's service   23
  method   23
  offer notices   22–3
  prospective purchaser notice   52
  time   23
Several buildings   20–2, 57

Severance of buildings
   service charge 21–2
   title 22
Shorthold tenancy, protected 12–13
Sports facilities 44–5
Sub-sales
   assignment of benefit of contract 12
   sale to sub-purchaser 12
   transfer of land to nominee 12
Subsequent purchasers, rights of tenants
    against
   disposal of part 50
   original purchaser 49–50, 145
   service of notice 49
Sub-tenancies 11–12
Surrender by landlord 47–8, 138–9
   notice for new lease 138–9
   other property included 48
Surrender of tenancy 16

Tenancies
   assured 13–14
   assured agricultural occupancy 13–14

Tenancies — *continued*
   business 13
   new, notice to purchaser requiring 144
   protected shorthold 12–13
   service occupancies 13
   surrender 16
Tenants, qualifying *see* Qualifying tenants
Time limits
   exercise of tenants' rights 41
   public auction 25, 26
   service of notices 23
Title
   land held under different 8–9
   severance of buildings 22

Undervalue transactions 16

Value change 47

Withdrawal
   deemed 33
   landlord 33, 128
   nominated person 34, 35, 129, 135